IN THE TANGANYIKA BUSH

Happy Hunting!

My Tanganyika Bush

IN THE TANGANYIKA BUSH

Stanley W. Hoffman

VANTAGE PRESS
New York

By the Same Author

Amid Perils Often

FIRST EDITION

Copyright © 1991 by Stanley W. Hoffman

Published by Vantage Press, Inc.
516 West 34th Street, New York, New York 10001

Manufactured in the United States of America
ISBN: 0-533-09354-6

Library of Congress Catalog Card No.: 90-91377

0 9 8 7 6 5 4 3

To

my son,

Kirk Randall,

who loves the African bush

as much as I do

Cush became the father of Nimrod; he was the first on earth to be a mighty man. He was a mighty hunter before the Lord.

—Genesis 10:8–9

As they were going through the vineyards there, he heard a young lion roaring. Suddenly the power of the Lord made Samson strong, and he tore the lion apart with his bare hands, as if it were a young goat.

—Judges 14:5–6

David said, "I take care of my father's sheep. Whenever a lion or a bear carries off a lamb, I go after it, attack it, and rescue the lamb. And if the lion or bear turns on me, I grab it by the throat and beat it to death. I have killed lions and bears."

—I Samuel 17:34–36

Contents

Preface

Ever since olden times man has pitted his strength against the wild beasts of the field. From these confrontations man has not always emerged the victor. On many occasions he lost the battle . . . and his life. Throughout the years game has been plentiful on the continent of Africa. It is only in recent times that there has been a rapid decline in their number. Some of this is due to the rise in poaching by the ever increasing human population. But mostly the animals have become silent victims to an all out slaughter by automatic weapons in the hands of rebels and soldiers who have been caught up in years of political upheaval and lawlessness of newly independent nations. Where will it end?

I am thankful for the privilege I had of entering the arena of man against beast during the tail end of those years when the hunter often became the hunted. It was a challenge to hunt the deadly Big Five, namely, the elephant, rhino, buffalo, lion, and leopard. Like Nimrod, Samson, and David before me, I pitted my strength against these beasts of Africa on their own turf in the Tanganyika bush.

From out of the past then emerge these true accounts of my wanderings in the Tanganyika bush. I took the liberty to relate them to you in the present tense so as to lend freshness.

Lastly, I am much indebted to my son, Mark, for proofreading the manuscript and then to my wife, Marion, who took time from her busy schedule to type it out so that I could send it on to the publisher.

Introduction

For years I have been sharing some of my hunting experiences while in the Tanganyika bush with those who were interested in listening to them. My children have heard them repeated countless times, I am sure. Yet years from now how much will they remember of their dad's safaris in the Tanganyika bush? This, then, is an endeavor to put down those experiences that I feel bear recording, not only for my children and their children, but for any of you who are interested in the life of a missionary who had the privilege of living in the Tanganyika bush, where game was still plentiful.

I spent fifteen years in Tanganyika (Tanzania), from 1959 to 1974, living at Kaiti in Mbugwe. The experiences recorded in this book are those I had while residing there. Never did I go on a professional hunting safari, as I was not a hunter by trade. In spite of that I was able to go at my leisure on many a hunt for meat or for just a time out in the bush away from the work.

The wild and the primitive have always appealed to me. Hunting thus was one way of escape from the busy modern world. I thank my Maker for keeping His protective hand on me, for without Him I am sure I would not be here today to tell you of those narrow escapes I have had.

While penning these experiences I am again there, feeling the tense moments, the heat, the thirst, the fatigue, and the thrill of the chase. These are memories, created years ago, to be enjoyed again and again. Come and walk along the paths I walked and stalk with me the animals I stalked. May you feel as I felt during those moments.

In my possession still is an old bush shirt, a pith helmet, my .458, and my hunting knife. Each time I come across these mementos, the present is blotted out and I again see the dancing heat waves out on the vast savanna, then, yonder, a herd of animals lazing in the shade of the acacia trees. My heart is ever where the baobab grows and where at twilight the black and white hornbill calls me "back, back, back" to the Tanganyika bush.

IN THE TANGANYIKA BUSH

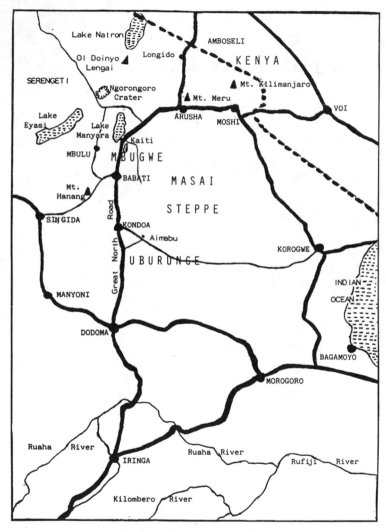

Tanzania (formerly Tanganyika)

Chapter One

An Ambush

A good many buffalo reside along the southern end of Lake Manyara. This is a marshy area with grass more than ten feet tall throughout the swamp, a regular haven for the buffalo to retreat into during the heat of the day. There they remain hidden among the dense vegetation, coming out to feed at dusk and during the night. They are heavily built, weighing up to a ton, and carry very massive horns. Peaceful when unmolested, they are extremely dangerous when cornered or wounded! Many hunters consider them the most dangerous of all game.

There are those of the Mbugwe tribe who dare to penetrate the dense, marshy bog and kill a buffalo or two with their spears. Most of the time these hunters will return un-scathed. But there are times when someone does get tossed or gored and he has to be carried home, either dead or badly injured. The wounded are usually taken to our mission dispensary for treatment and recover when brought before infection sets in. I recall one case where this did not take place. The ugly hole in the man's groin where the buffalo's horn entered was septic and full of matter. He had almost postponed it too long.

I have hunted buff in various kinds of cover, and it is risky each time. Though they are enormous, you often do not see much to shoot at, as they are able to conceal themselves very well. The ideal is to come upon them when they are out in the clear. This means an early start, catching them before they enter the swamp or settle down in tight bush. In the evenings they emerge as well, but your time is limited due to the approaching darkness. The light goes out quickly! There is no lingering twilight in the Manyara *mbuga* (swamp).

Their sense of smell is highly developed, while sight and hearing not as much. Keeping this in mind and timing it right, I have been able to close in on them adequately for a successful shot. Should I need a second or third shot, I will have ample time for it before they vanish into the tall grass. But in the best of circumstances there are times when your well-laid strategy does not come off as planned. That is why when one goes hunting big game, especially one of the Big Five, it can become dangerous and at the same time adventuresome!

Looking over a herd of nearly twenty head out on the open flats, I spot one I want. He is rather grayish, lighter in color than all the rest. I have been able to approach them within shooting range. I would have rather had them farther away from the edge of the swamp, but if I wait any longer they will retreat into it altogether, as dawn has already broken. He is standing broadside to me when the .458 slug slams into him. A well-placed shot, I thought, but he does not go down. The herd quickly stampedes into the swamp, disappearing into the tall grass with the wounded one in there somewhere. There was not another occasion for a clear shot. This now means I have to go in after him.

You just do not leave a wounded *nyati* (buffalo) to roam about. I have seen what they can do. A hunter had come out from Arusha and in the process of hunting game in the Lake Burungi area shot and wounded a big buffalo. The tracker, a local chap, said they had gone after the animal but finally called it off when the hunter ran out of time. There was now a mean old beast with a splintered front leg hiding out in the thickets looking for revenge. Biding his time, he was getting meaner by the hour.

Charcoal makers live along the edge of the Tarangire forest. They venture into it for the trees they need and return before dark to their homes. One night a man does not show up. His wife, thinking he has gone to a drinking party, does not give it much thought. *Pombe* (native beer) parties usually last all night. But when the following evening he still has not returned she reports it to a neighbor. The search begins in the morning. In an hour they find his remains. A messenger is sent to his wife and another one to the mission.

I take several students and a fellow missionary with me to the scene, a distance of only two miles. I have been asked to perform the last rites. It was not hard to see what had happened. The wounded buffalo had heard the man cutting wood and upon investigating had spied the human. The man must have noticed Nyati charging him and made for the nearest tree. But the thorn tree was neither tall nor sturdy, and the buffalo had knocked him out of the flimsy branches. Part of the man's clothing had snagged on the thorns and remained hanging in the tree. The woodcutter could not outrun the crippled buffalo and got only fifteen feet from the tree when he was hit. We see where the infuriated animal had vented his rage on the helpless human. He had knelt over him and commenced crushing him to death. He smashed the man's skull and caved in his rib cage.

A day later a leopard caught the scent of the dead and before long was feeding on the corpse, seeking out the internal organs. Had the remains been left out one more night we would have had nothing to bury, for surely the hyenas would have made the discovery. The hole the men have dug in the hard-baked ground is shallow, but big enough to deposit into it the severed limbs and the bits and pieces that were left of what was once a strong man, who had just a few days earlier called in at the mission. After the hole is covered, thorn branches are heaped over it to discourage the hyenas from digging up the remains. During the short funeral service the wife of the dead man stands silent and tearless. But I felt the tears were there inside.

Leaving the scene which had earlier been an arena of death, I wondered how many would find this exact spot in a few months from now. We had buried him out here where he had fallen—out in the Tanganyika bush.

Now here I am with a wounded *nyati* of my own. I know I have to go into that jungle of tall grass and finish off the gray bull I have just wounded. I am not going to be the cause of someone's death! Taking two of the men who have volunteered to accompany me into the swamp, I set out to follow the tracks the buffalo have left. Immediately we discover spots of blood on the trampled reeds. We cautiously stalk on, with me leading the way.

All is quiet. They are ahead of us somewhere. The reeds stretch high above me. It is impossible to see more then a few feet in either direction. The sun is heating up, and soon we will be sweltering in here. The tracks lead on, with one or two branching off now and then from the main herd. We no longer find any blood on the trail. It could easily have been covered with mud from the trampling hooves. There is some water, but not much. If any of them move we should hear them sloshing about. But there is no sound! I am now perspiring freely, and it is getting into my eyes. Just what I don't need!

We enter into a small opening, and there stand several buffalo. One of them looks just like the one I have wounded. He is grayish in color and is standing broadside to me with his head lowered. There is no bloodstain on him, but it is his other side I had hit. How can I make sure? Another buffalo is standing almost between us, only twenty feet away. Then there are others to my left and to my right. I can just make out their dark forms through the reeds. They are all too close for any shooting. If there is a stampede, we will be trampled into the mud!

We stand still and watch them. And they stand still and watch us. It feels like the inside of an oven. My shirt is soaking wet. The two men with me look scared. Who wouldn't be? We are in a tense situation. It could explode at any moment! Who is to make the first move? I decide I had better.

As I shoot past the beast standing twenty feet from me, the buffalo I have picked as the wounded animal goes down as if clubbed! None of the others move, including the one nearest to me. And a good thing they do not, for I am now grasping an empty rifle! The last shot has kicked open the clip, and the bullets have slid out into the water at my feet. I quickly slip a shell into the chamber and am ready for at least one more shot. I dare not fill the clip, as my cartridges may just get dumped again.

It isn't long and I hear steps behind me in the reeds. Only a few and then more. They are not moving away but drawing nearer! Are they going to form a circle around us? It is time now to make a hasty retreat, while there is a chance of getting out before we are surrounded by them. We back away ever so slowly, careful not to disturb those in front of us and beside us. A tense situation has now become extremely dangerous. My senses are becoming keener by the minute. I can hear the buffalo breathing down the nape of my neck where the sweat is now rolling freely.

Moving rapidly whenever there is shuffling of their feet in the bog and then cautiously when they stand still, we are able to cover ground without their knowledge. There is no breeze to assist them, nor us. Then we are beside one of them! I can just hear his heart beating. Or is it mine? The reeds com-

5

pletely hide us from each other. Holding our breath we edge past him, the grass whispering only slightly. Then we are on the tracks we had been on earlier after entering the swamp. With all the buffalo behind us we now increase our pace. Following the trail, we finally come out on dry land, much to our relief.

I know I have one dead buffalo in there and hope it is the one I wounded at the beginning of this hunt. Must give the herd time to disperse before returning in there for the dead beast. So we drive on home, and at four in the afternoon I find myself back at the *mbuga* once more. Brought with me a dozen men from the Bible School to help carry out the meat. They now follow me into the swamp. We walk in single file, talking and creating as much noise as possible. If any buffalo are lingering about, this should spook them away.

When we reach the dead buffalo, we find the rest have all disappeared. We cut up the beast so that it can be transported out on our heads or shoulders. Even the skull, complete with the horns, is to be lugged out to the vehicle. While we are slaughtering the animal I discover this is not the buffalo I had wounded out on the plain. Where is he? I had seen blood on the trail going into the swamp. He is still in here! It is no wonder this one did not charge us when we came upon them in the swamp. He had just looked at us. There was no reason to charge, for he was not wounded.

The hour is late, just enough time to get home before dark. The next day the wounded buffalo is located. He is grayish in color, lying dead beside the trail in the swamp. It is at the spot where we heard the buffalo breathing next to us just before stepping on the trail. Had he been waiting for someone to come along? Was he preparing an ambush for me?

Chapter Two

Will I Survive?

Jerry, one of my close friends, lives in Arusha, seventy-five miles northeast of Kaiti. He comes out once in a while to do some hunting for meat. We have walked many miles together in the Tanganyika bush. On his last outing he asked me whether I could back him in his first elephant hunt, to which I replied, "Sure, I'll accompany you for your first biggie." He remembers the date, and in the evening we make preparations for any early start out to Yaida Valley.

Yaida Valley is situated between the Rift Wall and Lake Eyasi and is a haven for elephants. It is rather remote geographically, with very few roads leading into it. The population is sparse, consisting mainly of the Watindiga. They are Bushmen, a remnant remaining from earlier years. Their livelihood is hunting for honey and meat, especially that of the elephant. The tsetse fly inhabits this isolated valley, preventing further human settlement.

I've hunted here for *tembo* (elephants) on previous occasions and have been successful on most safaris. For a quickie therefore, I thought, we'd best go to Yaida. If everything went well, we would be back by nightfall. If not, the day after for certain. In miles, distance wise, the valley is not that far, but the road we will be traveling to get there is atrocious. The escarpment at Magara will have to be scaled, then the

Mbulu highlands traversed on meandering roads before finally descending into Yaida Valley to commence our hunt.

We get our early start and soon are bumping over the jagged road in Jerry's Landrover. It is still dark when we ascend the escarpment. There are buffalo on one of the many switchbacks. They stare back in the headlights of the vehicle. When we finally switch off the Landrover in Yaida at a spot where we can survey the valley with our glasses, the sun has been up a couple of hours. Presently, we spot a herd of elephants lumbering aimlessly in the valley below. They are still feeding. We have arrived at a good hour.

We sit glassing them and waiting to see which way they will head, knowing that as soon as the midday heat increases they will halt for their siesta. It is usually under tall acacia trees, which offer the most shade and allow any breeze there may be to reach them. They then use their ears to cool themselves by fanning them. Once we know where they are planning to stop we will attempt to get there before they do.

Inspecting the herd through our binoculars, we discover the bull with the heaviest ivory. "He will do!" exclaims Jerry. Then something takes place that elephant hunters dream about but seldom see happen. The one with the biggest tusks, along with another bull, leaves the herd and strolls toward a hill! The others carry on up the valley in their relaxed gait. We note there are trees skirting the hill. "That's where they're heading," I said, and we then set out for them as well.

Leaving the vehicle, we descend to the valley floor. Keeping our eyes on the spot we last had seen the two, we strike off in that direction half running. Approaching the hill, we spy them at the tree line. Pausing to see which side of the hill they will select for their midday rest, we again have some good fortune. The two separate, one proceeding to the far side of the hill, and the second one, who happens to be the bigger bull, chooses the side nearer to us! We could not ask for a better setup.

8

The bull enters the grove of trees, and we hurry ahead to position ourselves for a decent shot, making sure we have the wind in our favor. At one point we are broadside to him, about one hundred feet away.

I whisper to Jerry, "You want to try him from here?" It is just right for a heart shot.

He declines. He explains that he had tested the rifle, which he had borrowed, and found that it was off target. "Can't we go any closer?" he asks.

"Sure," I answer. And why not? As long as he can keep his nerve I am willing to take him as close as he wants. I have been caught in close-ups before and have come out alive.

Before I purchased my .458, I rented a big gun each time I went after elephants. Going out for my first one back in 1960, I went to Lawrence and Downey and rented a double-barreled .500. I was asked whether I had ever shot an elephant before. I told the man that I hadn't yet. He took a postcard of a *tembo* and put a dot between the eye and the earhole. Another dot he placed on the animal's shoulder halfway up from the chest. "Here are the two broadside shots you take on an elephant," he told me. The latter one he advised me to take on my first hunt, as it could be taken at a distance of up to two hundred feet without failing to drop the animal under normal circumstances. The bullet would hit his leg bone, and his weight would break it. "Grounding him," the man called it. The elephant cannot maneuver on three legs and so collapses. You then go up to him and kill him in safety. "Of course," the man went on to say, "if you are not afraid then go right up to him and hit him between the eye and earhole or between the eyes when facing him. Make sure the angle is right, though, keeping in mind the brain is right between the earholes." That advice I have heeded throughout my hunting years.

We lose sight of the elephant as he goes deeper into the

trees. We scoot in a half circle, planning to come up just in front of him. There is a path and we get on it. The two Bushmen trail along behind us. No one wants a tracker in front of you when you are stalking. The Watindiga love meat and prefer to eat it raw. After shooting an impala or an eland, I have seen them cut off chunks of meat when they are skinning and commence eating it raw! The same is done with the animal's stomach, green juice running down both corners of their mouths.

The Watindiga hunt the elephant for meat. When coming up to a herd, they smear themselves with elephant dung so as to wipe out their own scent. Then they run up to one and cut his hind leg tendons. The animal is anchored and soon drops from spear wounds in his stomach. The whole village then camps at the carcass until it is eaten. There is much gorging, which lasts throughout the night. Our trackers are anticipating a lot of meat today.

We see the elephant ahead of us, just off the path we are using. He is standing under an acacia tree, reaching up with his trunk to pull off some green shoots. He does not know we are around. It's going to be easy! I take Jerry to within ten paces while the Bushmen remain behind. The bull is just off center to us. This means we need to move over somewhat, either to the left or to the right—to the left to get a side shot on the brain, to the right to get him between the eyes. In testing the breeze with some dust we learn that it is better to our left, where it will be drifting directly to us.

We move off the path to our left. After we take several steps, the angle is about right for a side shot. We are close enough to him now that he could pick up our movements at any time. I motion over to Jerry to shoot. He moves off the safety on his rifle, and it clicks! It is loud enough for the bull to hear the sound. He stops browsing immediately.

The elephant's head was broadside to us a moment ago,

but now it is swinging slowly to his right. He has guessed the direction all right and is peering our way. I hold my breath. Taking aim, I wait for Jerry's gun to explode. Nothing. The bull's head starts to move again slowly. Where are you, Jerry? I do not take my eyes off the animal's head. Still no shot! I quickly glance over, and Jerry is motioning for me to shoot. Looking back at the bull, I notice he is acting as if he is ready to turn and leave or else charge. I snap a shot at his forehead just as he moves it. Then, for the first time today, something does not go right!

The bull takes the bullet in his head, but not where I had planned it to go. Just a shade off. The head goes back, and he screams mightily, a sound which has to be heard to fathom its depth. It is spine-chilling! It is said that even the king of beasts, the lion, halts in midstride when the elephant speaks. As well, no other sound can so move a person. This is what it does to Jerry and the two Bushmen. They move! And leave me with a wounded elephant. He brings his head down and charges, the bush yielding him the right-away.

He is big! Now is a perfect head-on shot. I had gotten one like this before. He had practically been on top of me, blood showing on the side of his head from my previous shot. His trunk was extended, and he was trumpeting. My second bullet caught him in midstride, and he stopped as if he had hit a stone wall. He keeled over sideways, uprooting a tree as he fell two paces in front of me.

There is a difference this time. The difference is that I am holding an empty rifle! When I made my first shot I felt something brush against my fingers. Looking down, I see the clip has opened and all my bullets have dropped out. I am looking at an empty gun! It had done this once before, after buffalo. (I have fixed it since by hammering the catch so that it cannot open at all. I have to eject the cartridges now in order to empty the clip.)

11

I stand facing the charging elephant. His screams are deafening. I behold him coming at me in slow motion. My mind has now kicked into overdrive. Around in my head tumbles the question: *Will I survive?* I had heard of a few who had survived an elephant's charge by landing on a treetop where they had been thrown. Will I survive?

I have no time to pull a cartridge from my belt. I stand transfixed as he draws nearer. He keeps to the path and crashes by me, so close I could have touched him! Had I moved but a fraction he would have noticed me. He turns after he has gone seventy-five feet and is on his way around to return when my bullet hits him in the shoulder, grounding him. After he had gone by me I had enough sense left to pluck out a cartridge and stick it into the barrel and was ready to fire when he turned, which I knew he would do once he had the breeze in his favor.

Now all this transpired in less then twenty seconds! It takes much longer to relate it, of course.

I approach the fallen giant. There had been some thrashing and groaning, but he is now still. I find him dead. My bullet had found a vital organ. Then I hear my name called from a distance! It is Jerry. After hearing my second shot, he knows I am still alive. He is a relieved man when he arrives. He apologizes profusely for running out on me. I chalk it up as his first go at a "biggie."

During the cutting out of the tusks, the two Bushmen reenact Jerry's flight through the bush. They said he ran so fast they were left far behind. He gets back at them by relating how they had tried to climb a tree—a baobab at that!

After removing one of the tusks, we notice the lead of a bullet hanging inside the hollow part of it. The nerve inside is all festered. The elephant had taken the bullet fired by some hunter on a previous occasion. No wonder he came at me with revenge in his heart. He was going to make sure this human was not going to get away.

Looking back, I can see that had we not moved off the path several steps when we were lining up for a shot, I would not have survived!

Chapter Three

Charged

An animal that shows up at the most inconvenient moment is the rhinoceros. He is least wanted, especially when you are out after elephant. This is the time you need absolute quietness, no unnecessary noise. But so often the case has been that as I am approaching a herd, a rhinoceros charges out suddenly from behind a baobab tree or a termite mound! It is up to me then to do some fancy legwork to avoid being trampled or driven through with his horn. On many a hunt I have had to change my direction in a split second to avert being bowled over.

Not only will the rhino charge while you are afoot, but he will also rise to the challenge when you are driving a vehicle. There have been numerous occasions when this beast has persistently dogged me for long distances before tiring of the chase. On one such encounter the passengers in the back seat nearly crawled into the front upon seeing the huffing and puffing rhino just outside the rear door and only inches away with his menacing horn. We soon outdistanced him and the gang settled down and acted civilized once more. The children enjoyed these meetings whenever I would have just them with me. Their mother usually was not that keen in having a rhino lumbering alongside who suddenly would swerve to charge, barely missing the side of the vehicle.

The ending to some of my encounters with rhino while driving may have been entirely different had the vehicle hung up on a hidden log during my flight through the bush. He would have had the strength to flip the vehicle over, and if he chose not to, then he would at least leave as many dents and holes in it as possible. Rhino have enormous strength and have been known to charge and upset lorries (trucks). Even locomotives have been attacked and derailed by this powerful beast. Mind you, often this outburst of violent fury has cost him his life when pitted against a locomotive steaming down on him at great speed.

The black rhino stands five feet tall at the shoulder and weighs approximately three thousand pounds. In spite of his bulk, a *kifaru* (rhino) shows extraordinary agility, being able to turn on the spot. The front horn projects forward while the rear horn is much smaller. He is very shortsighted, but possesses a good sense of smell, which he relies on almost entirely. The rhino is ill-tempered and frequently charges without any apparent reason. His usual gait is a fast walk, with a bouncing trot when frightened. When charging he gallops, reaching thirty miles an hour for a short distance. As the rhino begins to charge he emits a puffing snort, repeating it several times.

We are working our way up to a herd of elephants which are just over the rise. Tramping along a path, all strung out in single file, we are startled by a loud snort ahead of us. Before we can collect our thoughts, a rhino comes puffing down upon us! The tracker who is ahead of me jumps out of the way, and I follow suit. I stumble on the stones and fall facedown beside the path, bruising my knuckles in the process, as I had quickly cradled my gun. Knuckles will always heal, but a rifle is hard to repair! The rhino rumbles on by. My hunting companion, walking directly behind me, is able to get off the path in time as well. But the two skinners tagging after him have turned instead and are fleeing down the path with the rhino

15

in hot pursuit. The slapping of the sandals on the soles of their feet can be heard fading into the distance intermingled with the puffing of the rhino. And then there is silence.

Sitting there, we wonder whether they have outrun the angry rhino. We continue to wait. Finally we see them stumbling back up the path. They are out of breath and ashen in color. One is really shook up and is unable to talk for some time. When his senses return to normal he refuses to go any farther with us and thereupon turns and starts back to his home. He has had enough!

It was next to impossible to purchase a license for a *kifaru* during my hunting days in Tanganyika. Therefore, whenever I entered the bush to hunt or to hike and the rhino charged, the onus was on me, not him, to come out of the encounter unscathed! These meetings, and there were many of them, were very lopsided, to say the least. There were numerous close calls. The risks would have been lessened had I had a permit or permission to shoot the beast. But since this was not the case *I* had to scramble to save *my* hide.

I should at this juncture mention that I did get permission from the Game Department to shoot one. Rhino were quite plentiful in our area, and eventually several made a nuisance of themselves. They would chase children who were on their way to or from school. Callers on foot coming to visit us would meet them on the path. When the residents complained to the Game Department, the scouts came and killed one less than a mile from the station. They were after another one, they stated. I volunteered to get that one for them. They consented, but I was to turn in the two horns.

The opportunity presents itself one hot afternoon. A fisherman from the lake on his way to our dispensary comes across the rhino standing in the shade of a tree near our compound. He storms to my door with the news. When I ask him to take me to the rhino, he entreats me not to go without my

16

gun. I was planning to leave it behind, wanting first to check if the rhino is actually there. I relent and carry the big .458 with me. The man then lights out with me at his heels.

Outside our compound is a fig tree with several palm trees near it. The fisherman is leading me to it, as it was under the fig tree that he had spotted the rhino. We approach the tree gingerly. The gentle, hot breeze is on my back. I do not like that. When the tree is in full view, we notice Kifaru is no longer there. As I begin to relax, the rhino charges from behind one of the palm trees on my right. He has switched trees! The fisherman comes by me in full flight. My heart is in my throat, and my legs tug to join the fleeing man. Had I not done this scores of times before? Hard to shake an old habit.

Finally reason prevails. I have a gun and have permission to shoot. Pointing the .458 at the rhino's head, which is almost at the end of my barrel, I pull the trigger. He keels over at my feet! It all happens so quickly! There had not been any time to raise the rifle and aim my shot. But it has been good enough. Now had I turned to run, I would never have escaped his horn. It was all too close and too quick.

*   *   *

Only twice have I ever had the thought come to me while facing a charge that I may not make it—once when I was facing a wounded elephant with an empty rifle and then when I was facing a charging rhino. I was backup for Simon, who was taking a friend out on a buffalo hunt in the bush near Lake Burungi. Though plentiful here, the buffalo are wary and difficult to find out in the open. We had left the vehicle behind and were now on foot.

Most of the forenoon we trudge the heavy woodland, checking one bluff after another. With the sun streaming down on us it is certain we will not find any out in the open.

They now are hidden deep in the heavy undergrowth where there is shade for them. There just were not enough reasons for any of us to stroll into their hideout for a trophy.

While we are crossing an opening a rhino charges us from behind a large termite mound which we are in the process of passing. We all scatter. Everyone for himself! I swing to my right, intending to place the anthill between the rhino and myself. Surely he will not veer that much and go after me? A rhino's charge is usually in a straight line, and woe to the person who happens to be in front of him. Therefore I should be quite safe, at least more so than the rest.

Hustling to skirt the mound, I take a quick glance over my shoulder at what is happening to the rest. There right behind me is the rhino! His snout and horn are just inches from my backside. I am flabbergasted! How did this happen? I turn to look ahead, but too late. I trip over a dead branch. As I go down in front of the charging rhino, I cry out, "Help!" I want the attention of the others, since they are safe. Will they be able to kill the animal before I am crushed to death?

While falling I twist to one side. This I habitually do so as to save the rifle from getting damaged. This time it saves *my* life! The wrinkled foot of the rhino lands where my body should now be. I glimpse the gray mass lumbering by, his loud puffing ringing in my ears. He stops short a few yards away, realizing I have dropped out of sight. Turning around, he sizes up the situation.

Meanwhile I have crawled behind the anthill. I am now hidden from his view. My two friends, I notice, are hiding behind some thorn trees a short distance away. The rhino now makes a few short charges, trying to pick up the scent of his intended victim. Giving up finally, he trots off, his tail pointing skyward. I had very nearly been trampled to death by him! I learned that day that a charging rhino can change course quite suddenly when he wishes to.

Chapter Four

Snared

The most powerful of the flesheaters is the lion. He has no natural enemy except man. The lion preys on various herbivorous animals. Young hippo and full grown buffalo are killed when lions attack as a pride. I have also come across a kill they made at a water hole, where a young elephant was their victim. Lionesses do the killing more frequently than the males. When fed, the lions constitute no immediate threat to the intruder.

They spend the heat of the day sleeping under the trees and do their hunting just before or in the dark. The grunting or panting of the lion can be heard while he is still in the distance. Then gradually it gets louder as he approaches. There is something about this sound in the night that makes Africa, Africa to me! We had no problem with thieves at night due to the prowling lions and leopards in the vicinity.

Lions are difficult to see in the grass during the dry season, they blend together so well. When one wished to walk to the lake, a couple of miles away from our station, one had to proceed through much tall grass. I did it many times. On one of these jaunts, I was hailed by a fellow up in a dry tree cutting off limbs for firewood. He inquired whether I had spotted the lions. I answered him, "What lions?" He went on to tell me that I had walked right by them! I wonder how often

I had done this in my previous treks. Unless you disturb them at midday, they are willing to leave you alone. Coming near an old, crippled lion who has not had anything to eat for days is, of course, another story. He will not hesitate to break your neck.

*   *   *

Two Masai warriors wandering across the savanna, less than two miles from our station, come face to face with a lone male lion. What good fortune! Here now was an opportunity to prove to their clan that they have the right to be called *il morani* (the warriors)! How often they have sat and heard their elders boast of how they had searched out the King of Beasts and then rushed him with their spears. Of course, the lion had fought back fiercely, but he had been no match for the warriors. Soon they were carrying the carcass back to their *boma* (stockaded village). There had then followed much singing by the young maidens, praising their heroes for their great courage. Today their turn has come to prove their manhood on the field of battle!

The two young men approach the lion cautiously. Simba (lion) does not bound off into the patches of long, dry grass, but continues to face them. One warrior turns to his left while his companion moves over to his right. If they can keep the lion between them they should come out of this all right, for should the animal charge the one, the other one will then rush in and drive his spear home. Only cowards cast their spears; so say the *morani*.

The lion does not wait until the warriors have taken up their positions. With only one flick of his tail and letting out a roar from deep down in his chest, which is enough to drain the courage of any stout fellow, he charges the one nearest to him. Rearing up on his hind feet, he knocks the spear aside and embraces the Masai. His jaws close on the man's throat, the teeth entering just behind his windpipe. But before he can rip out the man's life, a spear from the second warrior, who has come in from behind, enters his own body. The lion releases the man and seeks refuge in the nearby cover, the spear stuck deep in his side.

If the wounded man is to survive, his companion must quickly assist him to a doctor. After he is repaired at our dispensary, Gordon, a fellow missionary, offers to accompany them back to the arena. The *morani* is anxious to recover his spear.

The three approach the clump of grass where the lion had entered. Gordon has his rifle ready should the animal suddenly break cover. Then again, he may not be there anymore. To be certain, a few clods of soil are tossed into the dry grass. No answering growl. Only silence. Finally, they inch their way into the enclosure. Then they spot the back end of the lion. He is jammed underneath a fallen tree. Simba is dead. They discover that by diving under the log, he drove the spear farther into his own body as the shaft's end dug into the ground. It just as easily could have ended differently.

*   *   *

What about man-eaters, lions who have taken a fancy to killing and eating humans? Personally, I have not met one who solely sought me out so as to add me to his menu. But this does not mean that they were not there. Soon after our arrival in 1959, various accounts of man-eating lions terrorizing villagers in other parts of Tanganyika, especially during the first half of the twentieth century, did reach our ears. Someone from Singida shared with me how the man-eaters in that district included many of his tribesmen, the Wanyaturu, in their diet.

I will not take the time to relate to you encounters that others have had with man-eaters. There are books which have been written by those who have had the experience of dealing with them. But before closing this subject, I do want to leave you this account, as it took place only thirty miles from our station and just a few years previous to our coming.

The Great North Road, after passing through the Masai plains south of Arusha, climbs up an escarpment at the Essimingor range of mountains. (By the way, I have searched these hills for elephants carrying good tusks, but always in vain.) Here, at one time, crouching among theses rocks, lions kept a vigil after sunset for traffic coming up the incline. When an open lorry, carrying goods and *watu* (people) in back, came grinding along in first gear, they prepared themselves for the leap. At the right moment, one or two lions sprang onto the slow-moving vehicle and commenced lightening the load. When they each had a sleeping victim by the throat, they leapt off into the dark. It being nighttime, the driver and those inside the cab were often unaware of what was taking place until, reaching their destination, they discovered to their horror that some of their crew members were missing!

This section of road became so dangerous after dark that travelers with open vehicles made sure they left Arusha for points south in plenty of time in order to make it through the Masai steppe before nightfall. I could not help but give those same rocks the once-over, making sure my arm was not sticking out too far, each time I crawled up this particular stretch in low gear. Who knows? There may be a few offspring out there wishing to carry on the family tradition of the lions of Essimingor!

*   *   *

Lions can make you feel puny and helpless when you are

without a gun and surrounded by them. We were thus intimidated on a camp-out in Amboseli. The family and I had just completed our vacation on the beach at Mombasa and were now on our way home. Night finds us in our tent out on the dusty plains of the aforementioned park.

We had not yet dropped off to sleep when we heard the lions prowling around our tent. Their grunting had at first been distant, but then they drew nearer and nearer. Now they are just outside! What do they want here anyway?

It is cool tonight, but suddenly we feel colder. The children snuggle up closer to us in their sleeping bags. Outside we hear the lions making their rounds. Now and then they stop and all is quiet for a while. Then it dawns on me why they are hanging around! They are smelling the seashells we brought with us from the coast, that Marion and the children had picked. Most of them had not yet been cleaned, a chore left for when we get home. The shells are now up on the roof carrier of the Landcruiser, which is parked near our tent. Will the lions climb up there?

They are getting agitated. Their grunts are turning into growls. One stops where I am lying motionless. Will he paw his way inside? And me without a gun to protect myself and the rest. I hear his breathing. His mouth is open and there is a rasping sound deep in his throat. It is only twelve inches from my head, just a canvas separating the two of us!

Is our end to come in this manner? All because of some stinky seashells! I can see the headlines in the papers: "Missionary Family Mauled to Death by Lions in Search of Seashells."

The lion beside me finally moves away. They continue their snooping for an hour. Then all is still. They have gone. Our seashells are still there in the morning. They had not discovered them.

*   *   *

Our workmen have commenced working on a ditch which we are digging to help divert water so that the river will not flood its banks onto the station during the rainy season. This morning, they sight a lion nearby and come running to inform me. They shout excitedly, "Simba! Simba!" Taking our rifles, Gordon and I set out to investigate. It does not take us long to locate Simba. He and his mate happen to be feeding on a waterbuck they have killed next to our waterhole in the riverbed. As they are too well hidden for a good shot from where we discover them, due to thick undergrowth, we circle around and approach them from another angle.

As the male rises to face us, we shoot him from twenty yards. He sinks down lifeless without taking a step. The lioness looks befuddled, not perceiving what has taken place. The shots did not disturb her at all. We wait for her to charge and avenge her mate. But she does not! Instead she turns broadside to us and walks leisurely away! Not once did she stop or look back.

The lion is brought to the station and then taken on to the Game Department in Arusha. Of course, the workmen are disappointed that we did not kill the lioness as well. But when she cooperated so well by leaving, I did not have the heart to shoot her. One is enough as a warning for others to not approach too closely to our work camp. What about the remains of the waterbuck, of which there was quite a bit? The workmen ate that for lunch!

*   *   *

One of the ways the African obtains meat for the pot is by setting snares. But frequently a lion or leopard will get caught in one, which not only endangers the trapper's own life, but others as well, should the animal escape, snare and all. For that reason I would dismantle and remove any snares I discovered in my wanderings through the bush.

Walking past a dead, fallen tree, a lioness steps into a snare. The harder she tugs, the tighter the snare becomes around her paw. She cannot release herself from the wire which is holding her. Her mate stands by helpless, as does the other lioness. But they faithfully hang around, not anxious to forsake her. In desperation, the ensnared lioness begins chewing her paw in an endeavor to free herself. This brave attempt will not obtain her freedom, as she is operating on the wrong side of the snare!

The man who has set the snare for a zebra finally appears on the scene. At a glance he sees what has happened. His lone spear cannot accomplish much in this dangerous situation. Already the lion and lioness show signs of anger. What should he do? Leave and forget about it? After all, his puny spear is not enough. Maybe he should go and seek help? There is a white man with a gun not far from here.

I have my rifle as we draw near to the spot where he has left the doomed animal. Because of the clumps of trees, I do not notice the lioness until I am quite near her. She stands erect and starts to move off, but stops short when the fallen tree she is attached to, with the snare, will not budge. I slip out of the jeep and away from Marion and the children. The second lioness then stands up and confronts me. She has been hiding behind the fallen free. Then I see the male. He is off to one side, lying down and watching me.

What will happen after I put the ensnared lioness out of her misery? Will the other lioness charge? What about the male? I really only want to kill the wounded beast, no more. Will the other two cooperate and leave peacefully? We stare at each other. First I look at one and then at the other. They wait for me to make the first move.

I shoot twice and kill the one with the snare. The remaining two do not take their eyes off me. We watch one another. The lioness twitches her tail. The male blinks his eyes. More silence. Then slowly the old male turns and walks slowly away as if to say, "Well, that's over with." He has concluded that his mate was doomed and has recognized that I have done them a favor. The lioness soon follows the male when she discovers I am not interested in them. I begin breathing again. It had been a close scrape.

The lioness ends up at the Game Department as well. Didn't have a license for her. They were not that easy to get in Tanganyika at the time. Turned in the snare as well, but not its owner.

Chapter Five

Missed by a Whisker

I remember the first time I stared a *chui* (leopard) in the face. We had just taken up residence in our new station in the bush. The house had been erected quickly out of metal and aluminum sheets. There is an opening between the roof and the wall. Insects fly in and out freely. This opening also allows us to hear clearly the night noises all about us.

Something awakened me abruptly around midnight. My first thought was a rhino. I slid out of bed and crept to the window. I flicked on the torch (flashlight) and looked into the face of a leopard! There he sat outside the window, staring back at me. My knees went weak. I had my 30-30 in my hand, but it did not prevent me from shaking. It appeared to be too small right at the moment. I called Marion to come and look. It was barely a whisper. As we peered back at him, he switched his tail back and forth. He came erect gracefully and, without making a sound, slipped around the building out of sight. I was thrilled at what I had just seen, in spite of being surprised and visibly shaken by this midnight caller.

The leopard meanders along our riverbed nightly. Only his sawing cough coming from deep in his throat betrays his whereabouts. Then he is nearby, somewhere out there in the dark! He is a powerfully built animal, very agile, and more cunning than the lion. He preys on a wide range of mammals and often kills domestic stock. The leopard is solitary, except during mating season.

Chui is especially fond of dogs. He will go to any length to carry one off for a meal. Many a plantation manager has lost his favorite house dog or watchdog to the leopard. He has been known to steal into a bedroom and remove a German shepherd who was supposed to be watching, without a sound! The nearby owner sleeps through the whole performance. Although a leopard shies away from humans, he can become the most dangerous animal on earth should he turn into a man-eater!

We had a Pekingese named Mickey. He was our daughter's pet. At dusk the leopard would tempt Mickey to enter the grass outside our compound. The dog would bark and bark at the hidden leopard, who was luring him by purring. As soon as Mickey approached too near the grass line, we would take him indoors. Without our assistance, Colleen would certainly have lost her pet. Many a night Mickey would carry on barking for some time as the leopard sought a way to enter the metal building.

Following up a herd of Grant gazelles one afternoon, I am startled by a flash of spotted fur a few yards ahead of me. A leopard, hiding in an outcrop of rocks, chooses just then to spring on top of the male bringing up the rear. While in midair, the ambusher spots me for the first time. As soon as he lands on the gazelle, he spins around and streaks off among the rocks, leaving behind him the wounded animal. In spite of a sudden change of plans, made after takeoff, his claws still raked deeply the victim's back. It takes me half an hour to approach near enough to the now startled herd to complete the job I had interrupted. The meat really belongs to my spotted friend, and it would now be his, had I not intruded when I did.

*   *   *

Not far from our station a *chui* is caught in a snare. Of course, it had been set for an impala, but it is the leopard who gets there first. The owner of the snare comes for help. It is a risky undertaking.

He leads me into the palm forest where there is a stand of tall buffalo grass in a low depression. Pointing to it, he states that the leopard is in there somewhere. I scan the area and observe nothing that resembles the wild creature we are after. I listen and hear nothing. Wishing to know his whereabouts, I drive the vehicle slowly into the depression. Cannot see much from where I am sitting. Then there is a waving of grass in front of the vehicle. It leads away and then stops abruptly—less than ten paces ahead. It is the leopard. He has moved into this tall grass in order to hide. He has been able to drag the heavy branch, to which he is attached by a wire snare, into this hollow. But here his movements are hampered; the branch, hanging up against the tough reeds, allows him to move only short distances with each lunge.

I have others with me in the vehicle, including my wife and Kirk. They have come with me to see a quick execution, which now is turning into a drastic affair. Not wishing to involve them in an unpleasant ordeal, I decide to leave them parked in the vehicle near the edge of the depression while I walk in after the leopard. We have our movie camera along. Marion is to take pictures and guide me from her position.

Cautiously I wade through the grass, aiming at the spot where I last saw the leopard stop. I avoid the path he has taken. There is a trail of bent-over grass where he has fled. It would be suicide to follow that in, as he is waiting on the other end for me to approach! Then he would spring on me so quickly that I would not have a chance in a million to stop him with a bullet. It would be all over before I know what hit me. I would be no match against his fangs and claws. A white hunter and his gun bearer narrowly escaped death when they were mauled by a leopard in this very area. This happened just prior to our coming to live here.

I am moving in on the leopard at an angle. It is too quiet. He makes no sound. Then the grass stirs a little to my left. The leopard moves in fast, the grass parting in front of him. Just as quickly, he stops two paces away. I still cannot see him! He has miscalculated! Eager to get me, he has charged too soon. He did not allow himself enough lead and so comes up just a bit short. He may have reckoned that the branch would slip more over the grass when he pulled. But it has snagged fast. The leopard bounds off in the opposite direction, going as far as the snare allows him, and then all is quiet again.

I give up the fool notion of flushing him out while on foot, return to the waiting vehicle, and this time crawl onto the top of it for a better view. My friend then drives me back in after the leopard, leaving Marion behind on foot to take more movies. The approach is made from the opposite side. Suddenly he is running away from us. I can see him now. He is able to travel fifteen feet and then is brought up short by the branch when it anchors against the bunched grass. By my figures, this means anyone approaching the wounded leopard now within thirty feet would get mauled! His "leash" will permit him to rebound that much. That is not counting any footage he may gain should the branch hit a patch of limp grass.

Motion to the driver to move ahead. The branch is now only three paces away. Holler for him to stop as I see the leopard charge and brace myself for the shot. He comes full tilt. Sighting me, he springs. Shoot him in his open mouth, the end of the barrel an inch from his jaw.

What about Marion? Oh, she got a few pictures but was more engrossed in me not getting hurt. What if the leopard had come her way? I had not thought of that.

*   *   *

30

A hyena howls nearby as I pull up the dead reedbuck and then tie the rope to the base of the tree. The carcass is now five feet clear of the ground. The leopard will have to rear up or climb onto the limb if he is to feed on it. It is a fresh kill, purposely made two hours before sunset. I wanted the leopard to hear the shot and then come to investigate. He is now on his way, I am positive, as the hyena already has sprung the alarm that there has been a kill.

Many believe the meat has to be ripe before the leopard comes to the bait. But in my years of hunting I have had this spotted cat arrive within an hour or two after I make a kill in his immediate haunts. One day when I am returning with a zebra in the back of the jeep, a two-inch thorn finally works its way through and the tire goes flat. While I am replacing it with the spare, the children who are along spot a leopard slipping through the foot-high grass. He is heading our way.

He had heard the shot, then scented the blood, and now was approaching to investigate whether any of it would be available for him. Noticing that we are conscious of his whereabouts, he halts and flattens himself on the ground, peering at us with his large amber eyes. And then he is gone! Where did he go? No one saw him slip away, so well had he been camouflaged. My rifle is beside me and ready as I tighten the bolts on the wheel. Bouncing our way out of the bush, we do not catch a glimpse of him again. This does not mean that he is not out there within a stone's throw.

The bait that I have tied to the tree in front of me is to entice the big male leopard who has been sighted on numerous occasions snatching away goats from startled herd boys. It is almost dark now. For an hour I have been ready for him. Even though I do not see him or hear him, I feel he is nearby. I have a torch taped to the side of my 30-30, just in case I need it, should he wait until after dark to make his appearance. I hear the hyena again; he is much closer now than the last time. Surely the leopard will not allow the hyena to steal his meal?

I remember the time my colleague staked out a goat at Aimabu. When he heard the animal scream an hour after dark, he flicked on his torch and, spying a spotted form, shot. Instead of a dead leopard, he discovers he has killed a hyena. May the same thing not happen to me tonight.

I notice a movement down at the tree. It is quite dark, but I do detect an animal circling the bait. I must not wait any longer. In the light of the torch I see a magnificent male leopard. He is the one! He gives me a sideways glance, and I pull the trigger. What happens next is impossible to explain because he just disappears, vanishes, without me even catching any movement!

I shine my light around the area but do not see a leopard. Not going to move around out there in the dark, in case he is only wounded. But I am positive I hit him in the heart. Too close to miss. Keep up my vigil for some time, but when nothing more happens, I succumb to sleep. At the break of day, I discover the leopard. He did not go far, about twenty yards. The bullet had smashed his heart. With his last breath he was still able to dash that distance. What stamina!

*　　*　　*

While stationed in the scrubland of Uburunge, I hear the ululating of a herd boy late one afternoon. I have come to learn that this means a leopard has attacked one of the animals. The lad is putting up a gallant stand against this perfect killing machine, but all to no avail. I have to cross a ravine to get to the scene, and when I arrive, the leopard is gone and so is the goat. This happens over and over, as leopards are plentiful in Uburunge, located southeast of Kondoa.

A short time after this, a man from a mile up the road,

Salimu, arrives in the evening. He informs me that a leopard has just killed one of his cows. They have driven off the beast. Could I quickly come and shoot the leopard when he returns to the kill? The shadows are lengthening by the time I arrive at the site. Looking around, I spy a tree nearby of medium height with a fork in it. It is just what I want. Hurriedly we put up a couple of poles crossways in the fork, one for me to sit on and the other for a gun rest. After pulling the dead animal nearer to my tree, I climb into my perch twelve feet up. Salimu returns to his hut, where he lives with his two wives. Marion, who has come along, goes with him to await the outcome. I am now alone. Taping the torch to the side of my 30-06, I settle down to await the return of the leopard.

There is dry bush interspersed with small openings in three directions. Behind me is Salimu's *shamba* (field). If the leopard returns, it has to be from one of those three directions, where there is ample covering. As the last light is fading, I see him! He is a big male, very light in color. He stealthily slips from one cover to another. He is only twenty-five yards away and straight in front of me, yet leading off to my right, probably circling to investigate if all is well. I wait, expecting a quick encounter.

It gets darker and then I cannot see, not even the dead cow below. No moon to assist me. A breeze starts to stir, and I feel cold. I am wearing a short-sleeved shirt. I keep straining to hear the crunching of bone or the ripping of flesh commence, but nothing. I wait. Once I hear a slight rustle of grass below. That must be him! It will not be long now. After half an hour of no further sound, I conclude that it must have been a dik-dik crossing the glade.

At nine o'clock I am getting cramped from my crouching position. I need to shift into a different pose. Before I do so, I flick on my torch to see how it looks below. There, in the light, I see the leopard beneath me! He is lying beside the carcass and surveying me. That was him that had caused a slight rustle! He has been keeping his eye on me ever since. The kill lies untouched beside him.

Taking a bead on his head, I see two eyes and then only one glowing back at me. That puzzles me. He must be turning his head sideways. When two appear again, I fire, aiming between his eyes. The leopard vanishes! Where he had been lying just a second ago he now is no longer there. What has happened? I can hear no thrashing about on the ground near the tree. He should be sprawled dead or, at least, mortally wounded, waiting for me to finish him off. Is it safe to descend?

From the hut, my wife just then calls, "Are you all right?" I had better get down quickly before she and Salimu arrive. With a wounded leopard about, it is better he attacks me first. I slide down the tree and investigate the surrounding area with my torch. No leopard. Examine the ground for a sign of blood, but there is none. There is not much more I can do tonight. Too risky in the dark. Decide to resume the search in the morning. Meet my wife and Salimu on the way, we return home, hoping that the leopard will be found dead in the morning.

The next day we see what had happened. Where the leopard had been lying there stands a sapling, less than an inch in thickness. It was enough to blot out one eye when the leopard moved his head slightly to the side. As I had no knowledge of this and shot when I saw both eyes, the bullet, instead of hitting the leopard, glanced off the sapling. Had I shot when there was only the one eye, the leopard would now be dead.

The bullet, hitting the sapling to one side, veered sharply and in its flight seared off some whiskers from the leopard's face. We see the path it had taken through the bush by the nicked branches along the way. The claw marks are there, near the sapling, where the leopard had suddenly sprung to life and dashed off into the night. He was not even wounded. This is one of those times when you wish you could have another chance. You would do things just a bit differently. All it would have taken was just a bit!

Chapter Six

Shamba Raiders

In Uburunge, the inhabitants grow maize as their staple food. They are constantly forced to guard their crops against raiders if they plan to harvest anything. The bush pig can do a lot of damage, but the greatest of the *shamba* (cultivation) raiders is the elephant. A herd, even with only a few head, can wipe out a crop of maize in one night! I have witnessed the havoc they wrought in many of the Uburunge *shambas* during my work there.

Uburunge is hilly, bushy, and quite arid. There are no real forests in the district. The elephants have adapted themselves to living in the dry, scrubby bushland interspersed with cultivations. The gray beasts blend in well with their cover, which is just high and dense enough to hide them from any passing humans. They have become masters at concealing themselves.

Living in this type of an environment, the *shamba* raiders have become accustomed to being in close proximity with the cultivators. In fact, they are so used to them that they do not fear the humans and will not run no matter how much bedlam the people raise. The scent of man is no cause for alarm, only caution. Not really an attractive place to go elephant hunting!

I find myself on the trail of the raiders. The maize is in

The Author

An Eland

Feeding on Wild Figs in Our Backyard

A hunting we will go!

The Day the Tracker Almost Got Trampled

Switchbacks up the Escarpment from Magara

Mtindiga Hut in Yaida Valley

Our Mtindiga Guide, a Bushman

The Rogue Elephant

The Buff Who Refused to Leave the Swamp

The Old Buff Who Charged Us

The Snared Lioness

A Game Scout with His Dead Rhino

One of Many Termite Mounds

A Rhino I Did Not Run From

Glassing for Elephant in Yaida

Let's go get him!

My hat goes off to the herd bull.

The Baobab Tree we slept in

A Kongoni (Hartebeest)

A Wildebeest

A Lesser Kudu

A Bushbuck

"Unataka nini?" (What do you want?)

Chawing on Elephant Meat

ear now, and the elephants are savoring it. They are near a certain village a delegation had come from earlier asking for help. Would I shoot one of the animals so that the rest would then move off somewhere else? I agreed, with one condition, that I will shoot only a large tusker, so as not to waste my license on small stuff. I knew if I could not catch the raiders still in the *shamba* after dawn or on their way to feed in them before dusk, my task would change. I must then enter a dense thicket and shoot the biggest tusker there. Sounds simple, but it is like looking for the proverbial needle in a haystack!

Hunting *shamba* raiders involves the villagers. It is their maize that gets eaten and their crops that get trampled in the process. There is a troop of them anxious to go with me on the hunt. That is just what I do not want, a lot of people tagging along, all chattering and no one listening. After a stern lecture, a few turn back, but not all. The sun has been up for some time, and the elephants have retreated to their hideaway. We are able to pinpoint their whereabouts from information given by the owners of the *shambas* we have passed all along the way. Finally, we arrive at a stand of trees that holds the raiders.

Slipping from cover to cover, I notice most of the villagers are not taking the precaution that I am. As I motion to them to be quieter, they answer, "Oh, they already know we're here." And it is so! When we finally spot them, the elephants are huddled together facing us. In the tight, thorny bush we are no more then ten paces from them. For an hour we eye them. They do not move but continue to gaze back at us. Unless the herd breaks up, I will not be able to see those on the far side. I need to appraise their tusks before I can decide which one to drop.

While I am waiting, some of the villagers with me are starting to leave. I have been observing them glancing about for a tree high enough to climb, should an elephant decide to charge. Seeing that there are not any sturdy ones around, they are calling it quits. After all, they think, they each have a wife or two with children at home who need them. The troop commences to thin out, and only the hardy remain to brave it out to the end.

Noting that the elephants are not anxious to move and with the sun getting hotter, I decide to make a move myself. I am not prepared to baby-sit a herd of *tembo* in this inferno. Inching my way along, I am able to glimpse those standing behind the front line. Stare as I do, the tusks will not grow any longer! None of the raiders have ivory worthwhile shooting for the license. As I creep back out into the clearing, the men following do not know what has happened. Has the Bwana lost his nerve and gotten frightened? I explain that the tusks would not pay for my license. I can see by their expression, "So what?"

Walking along, I feel awful because they feel awful. The *shamba* raiders have gone unpunished. When I am about to leave the vicinity, a runner greets us with the news that another herd has been spotted about a mile from here. Our sagging spirits begin to soar. "Any big tuskers in the group?" What a foolish question to ask! Of course, the answer will be in the affirmative. "*Ndio, Bwana, refu sana!*" ("Yes, sir, very long!")

Feet that had been dragging suddenly become lighter as we move along to the location where the herd was last seen. The villagers along the way must have perceived that I would come, for they are preparing themselves for the meat they are going to eat come nightfall. The bush telephone beats any system we may have for communicating! I have had people come to me for a ride to town when I had not told a single person outside of my wife that I was even going! She and I had decided on the spur of the moment that we would go. This was at bedtime. We would leave at dawn. But who should be there when we are ready to leave? A passenger or two.

We branch off the main path and head for the trees, a short distance away. No need to be careful about which way the breeze is blowing, since the scent of man will not panic them. The one who brought us the news of the elephants is in front, and who knows how many are behind me? At each backward glance I see another one has attached himself to the column.

The trees are spaced farther apart in this bush, giving us a greater view. It does not take long before we spot them. They are moving along lazily, browsing among the branches. One of the men points out that this herd always stays in this immediate locality. It is nearer to the riverbed, and therefore the vegetation remains lush longer than farther up, near the hills. The villagers also raise better crops of maize here. This place, then, is a haven for the raiders.

As they stroll aimlessly through the wooded grove, I locate one that carries heavy tusks, the best ones I have seen in Uburunge thus far. I immediately strike out in his direction. Then the unexpected happens! An unsuspecting villager on his way through, without knowledge of us or the elephants, puts them on their guard. The *tembo* move off into cover again. We sprint forward, not wanting to lose them in the heavier bush farther on. To get to it they will have to pass through an opening ahead of us.

Then there they are. The big one is with them, and he is walking away. Only his back end is showing. If he gets into that tight brush, I may not obtain anything better for a target. I shoot for his backbone, just above the tail. It is a little low, for he speeds off with the rest. We rush after them, expecting to find him lying within the stand of trees. But there is nothing. There are branches breaking farther along in the bush. Do we follow their spoor or circle around and try to cut them off somewhere ahead? I decide on the latter.

49

I dash off. One villager sticks with me, while the rest stay. We skirt the tree line and then race for a point where I believe they will be passing. We warily enter the grove again. There is a slight depression ahead of us. Where there had been complete stillness now suddenly there is pandemonium! Trees begin swaying in front of us, and then the elephants stampede up the depression, straight for us. I snap off a quick shot near the head of the one closest to me! He veers, knocking the one on his left off stride as they surge past us. Trees are crashing, and branches are popping. We do not move until the dust has settled. That was close! Too close. That we avoided being trampled is a miracle.

Retracing our steps, we come across the rest of our party. They are wondering what has happened. Then I learn why the herd had stampeded. Some in the waiting party had gone into the bush to look whether the herd was still there. The now vigilant herd, with the wounded one in their midst, tore off in mad flight. We just happened to be in their path. No sense in doing any more today. Do not want to chase them out of the vicinity. Tomorrow we will return to search for the one I have wounded. He cannot go too far if left alone.

We meet women carrying baskets on their heads on the way back. They are crestfallen when told there is no meat. But wasn't there a big bang? (The report of an elephant gun carries a long distance.) I feel about two inches tall. Try explaining how come you missed! They believe every shot is a hit and every hit is a kill. I feel better the next day when the carcass of the wounded elephant is found. He had not gone far after being hit. He was not even with the stampeding herd. I have redeemed myself in the eyes of the expectant women.

*   *   *

Another morning, three villagers and I are following a

herd that has gone up into the hills after raiding a few *shambas*. Following their tracks from one bramble bush to another, we finally catch up to them. It is now near noon, and they are in a good-sized stand of trees with heavy under-growth. I drop to my knees and commence crawling. A couple join me. Ahead a twig snaps. Then the flapping of an ear. I still cannot see anything. A few yards to the left comes a rumble. Have I gone too far? We may now be in their midst! I pause.

Through the saplings ahead of me, a form slowly takes shape. There are others, but not as visible. Brush starts crackling to our side on the right, and then an elephant pushes his way into view. The dry branches scrape along his rough hide. He pays no attention to us and halts to pull some shoots off a green tree with his trunk. His tusks are not heavy. We wait for the others to disclose themselves. Minutes tick by.

Then more noise comes from almost directly behind us. I get ready. I will have to shoot if the elephant proceeds on course. I am sure he knows we are here. The rustling draws nearer. I still cannot see him. Finally, the undergrowth parts and a *man* creeps into view! Then one more comes up behind him. So intent are they in stalking the elephant to our right that they have not noticed us. The one in front carries a rifle. He is either a game scout or a poacher. If the latter, he may even shoot me for catching him in the act.

I had wanted to see what ivory there was in the herd, but now it looks as if these two are going to spoil it by blasting away at a reject. I have to act fast if I am going to do anything about it. As the man with the gun is ready to fire, I whistle loud enough for him to hear me. He glances over at me with a startled look and lowers his rifle.

After we have withdrawn from the bush, he informs me who he is. He claims he is hunting for a certain Mzungu (European) in Kondoa. When I ask him which one, since I know some of them, he cannot tell me. I conclude he is a poacher. His gun, an old model, testifies to it. What to do with him? He says he now wants to go back in and shoot the big one. I explain that he is not big, but the poacher will not agree. He says the elephant is very big, meaning his stature, of course. He was not really looking at his tusks, but just wants to shoot any elephant. The Waburunge eat the meat, and he could make just as much by selling the meat to them as by selling the ivory to one of Kondoa's many Arabs.

He finally agrees that I will look over the herd for a big tusker. If there is one, I will shoot it, take the ivory, and leave him the meat. Creeping back into the jungle of undergrowth, I feel someone close behind me. It is the poacher, the man with the rifle. He will not leave, so I resign myself to having him tag along. Each elephant we spot he wants to shoot. It is all I can do to control him. I do not desire his presence any longer, so I leave the bush and the elephants behind me. The fellow is just too trigger-happy!

He and his companion wish to accompany us for the rest of the day. I refuse and we part. But it is not long after when we spot them on our backtrail. They are following at a short distance. We make for the village. May as well call it a day, especially with a daffy on our backs. It is late afternoon when we touch the valley floor. The *shambas* lie beyond the bushes ahead of us. Before pushing on, we perch on the rocks to catch our breath. Sitting there, we again see the poachers. I wave them back. They duck out of sight.

Intersecting the wooded area are wide passageways. Proceeding along one of them, we encounter a herd of raiders on their way down to the *shambas*. We cannot believe it! Plus there is a nice tusker among them. They lumber across into the next cluster of trees. We hasten to intercept them on the other side. Some are out already when we get there. Where is the big one? Had he emerged first and gone on to another bush, or was he still inside? Then I spot him in the shadows. He is carrying enough ivory!

As I hurry to get closer to him for a better shot, a gun goes off behind me! A cold shiver runs up my spine as I hear the lead whine over my right shoulder. A quick glimpse back reveals that idiotic poacher with a raised gun! The herd has stopped and is now turning around to re-enter the bush. I have to act quickly if I am to obtain my *tembo*. I aim at the bull's shoulder and fire. He slumps down immediately, just at the fringe of the thicket. Rushing over, I put a bullet into his brain.

The poacher then comes up and has the nerve to say that he has shot the animal. Everyone there knows his bullet had gone high and off into the branches. He has said this so as to put a claim on some of the meat. He is not only getting on the villagers' nerves, but he is beginning to irritate me as well. I remind him that he almost killed me, instead, with his reckless shot! He claims I had moved in his way. He is impossible!

After the tusks have been dug out of the skull, I remain for the cutting up of the meat. I do not want to leave the villagers alone with the unreliable poacher. He would take over after I leave, claim the carcass, and then charge them for the meat they take. The villagers verify that this is what he would do. If anyone deserves the meat, it is the locals who have had their *shambas* raided by this animal. The two poachers finally move off after helping themselves to a hunk of meat.

Women have arrived with their containers and baskets. The men are hacking away at the carcass. *Pangas* (large knives) flash everywhere in the light of the fire, which has been built so they can see. There is great excitement, with much laughing and talking. Chunks of meat are draped on every branch. Soon they will hang the pieces on poles and carry them back to their villages. I am sitting here hunched in the shadows, chewing some roasted elephant meat and listening to them narrate of the fall of this great *shamba* raider!

Chapter Seven

The Rogue

My tracker and I are combing a wooded area in Uburunge for the spoor of a certain herd of elephants. They were supposed to have passed this way within the last day. We have been told that many carried big tusks. This is often the case. You hear what you want to hear:

"Are they big?"

"*Ndio*, Bwana."

"Are they near?"

"*Ndio*, Bwana."

"Are they still there?"

"*Ndio*, Bwana."

Then after traveling and walking for many miles, you arrive and are told by the locals that the elephants have just left!

While we are in the process of scouring the countryside for the elephants' tracks, a runner shows up with the news that a man has been killed by an elephant. Would I come and shoot the animal? Now should I believe this story?

"Where did it happen?"

"Just a mile or two away, Bwana."

"Is the man dead?"

"*Ndio, kabisa!*" ("Yes, completely!")

I guess the only right thing to do is go and find our whether a man was really killed. But it probably is not as near as he says.

It looks as if he has traveled a greater distance than that.

He guides us deeper into the wooded area, passing a *shamba* now and then en route. After bumping along for several miles, we arrive at a lonely hut just as the sun is touching the treetops. It will be dark before too long. A woman and three men come out to greet us. Yes, the husband of this woman was killed by an elephant during the night. It had happened while he was watching his maize in the *shamba*. So it really did happen!

We walk into the *shamba*, which lies behind the hut. The maize, what is left of it, is just beginning to ear. In the center of the field is a raised platform the owner had climbed upon to watch for wild pigs. Many times, pigs come in the night, push over the stalks, and eat the maize. But last night the man had an unexpected visitor, one of the worst kind, a rogue elephant!

A rogue elephant is usually a loner, kicked out by the herd because of his ill temperament, which may be due to a wound of some kind. The wound is inflicted by a hunter or poacher using too small a rifle or by a native spear or arrow. The afflicted area then festers and he is crazed with pain. Man did this to him! He is outraged at this puny being. Seeing one cross his path, he runs him down and smashes the life out of him—a way of getting even for the agony he carries with him in his wanderings.

The *shamba* raider, or marauder, by living in close proximity with the villagers will lose fear of man to the extent that he will turn on him when challenged. The missiles thrown at him while he is raiding someone's *shamba* only infuriate him, whereas an elephant in Yaida Valley pelted in like manner will dash off to cover. The enraged marauder here will kill the man should he persist in discomforting him. This may have been the case last night. Whichever way it was, there is a man-killer loose in the neighborhood! Will he return to this maize field tonight?

I examine the tracks made by the rogue. They are still distinguishable in spite of the many footprints made by humans since the fatal incident took place. We discover where the elephant has departed into the tall grass bordering the field. The telltale signs reveal that the man had attempted to drive off the animal when he entered the crop of maize. The rest must have happened quickly. I was told the body was badly mutilated and the remains had to be buried that morning. We decide to spend the night where we are. If the rogue does not return before morning, then I will go after him at daybreak.

He does not put in an appearance that evening, but in the morning we do find fresh spoor at the edge of the *shamba*. He had come, eaten some maize, and then wandered off toward the nearby dry thorn bushes. We now have a new set of tracks to follow. The tracker I have with me is good. Jerima has accompanied me on previous occasions, especially for greater kudu. He seems to know where the elephant will go and proceeds along at a good pace. Thus we make suitable time in tracking the rogue.

Since this morning we have been in brushy country. There are tight bushes scattered about with open meadowland in between them. The trees are not tall, but high enough to hide a *tembo*. The color of these bushes is such that they can easily camouflage an elephant in them. This means we have to stop and peer into the closely spaced trees for a sign of the rogue. He goes into one stand of trees, only to exit on the other side. He does this on several occasions as he seeks a place to put up when it gets too hot. It is midmorning when we fail to see any sign of his departure from the bush he has entered.

The tracker has done his job well. It is now my turn. Doing it once makes you think twice before going in after an elephant alone! I am doing it again today. Only this time it is after a rogue. I can still remember the last venture I had going in after an elephant that I could only hear but not see. This was back in Mbugwe. It was a heavily wooded area near a stream. The undergrowth was so thick and high that it was impossible to see in any direction. His stomach rumbles gave me an idea of his whereabouts. There could be others near him, but that was a chance I had to take. I soon came up to him, the soft grass and leafy branches making no noise as they brushed against me. Then I could see part of his head and his tusks. The ivory was good and I shot him. He fell where he had stood. Three others then broke loose in front of me and disappeared into the green entanglement.

Today I am going in on my hands and knees, as the brush is dry and would create too much noise against my clothing. By getting down and creeping along the path the rogue has taken, I can get away without making the slightest bit of sound. Just as long as he does not hear my heart pounding! To my ears it sounds like the tom-tom of a native drum.

His tracks are there, before me on the path. Creeping along, I lift one knee at a time, slowly and carefully. The rifle is palmed in my right hand. As I move it ahead, in my awkward position, I try to keep the grime from entering the barrel. There are trees to my left and to my right, but none high enough to give proper shade for a *tembo* at this time of the day. The hour is approaching when they usually like to halt for a siesta. Then something does not appear quite right!

When you are in tense situations, your senses become highly acute. Usually it is my hearing, but right now it is my sight. Three paces ahead of me I see a tree planted in the middle of the path I am on. How can that be? My stomach knots. Then it dawns on me: it is the front leg of the rogue! I do not breathe. Without moving, I glance upward. I cannot see the rest of him. He is well hidden from view.

I reverse cautiously. Then I spy a tree alongside of me to my left with a branch five feet off the ground. It appears sturdy enough to support my weight. Laying the rifle against the trunk, I inch myself onto it, and then I haul the .458 up after me. I am tempted to hurry, lest he moves away, but I know discretion is the better part right now. Rising up to my full height, I sight him.

The rogue is standing below me, his head less than twenty feet from the end of my rifle. He has not noticed me and is still facing his backtrail. His huge head is dipped slightly, ears extended, and he is peering intently at the path before him. He is waiting for me to make my appearance so that he can grab me with his trunk and then finish off this hunt in his favor. One more shove ahead with my knee was all he needed to add a second victim to his list in as many days. Thank God I had seen the "tree" in time!

I bring up the .458 slowly and cautiously with my right hand. I cannot grip it with both hands, as my left hand is grasping the tree. Any moment now, he may sense me. Bracing the gun against my side, I aim for his brain and squeeze the trigger. I cannot miss at this range.

The rogue does not know what hits him. He sags down and rests on all fours, his head nodding up and down. I have had them fall in this manner on previous occasions. This makes it a lot easier to dig out their tusks. But most of the time they come to rest on their sides, making it difficult to extract the bottom tusk. The skull must then be severed. Looking at the swaying head before me, I take a deep breath finally—for the rogue before me is dead.

Chapter Eight

Pursued

Many hippos congregate on the southern tip of Lake Manyara where it meets the Kou River. At dusk they leave the water and go foraging on pastures or in the lush green gardens of natives living in the vicinity. The entire day is spent resting on the banks or in the water. Hippos are semi-aquatic. They swim extremely well and dive for periods averaging two minutes, but can stay submerged for up to six minutes. Standing five feet at the shoulder, they average three thousand pounds and sometimes reach twice that weight.

Well after dark I have heard them grunt back and forth, interspersed occasionally with a bellow. The bulls are fierce fighters and frequently engage in combat, inflicting horrible wounds on each other with their teeth. They can even be dangerous to man, especially if he gets between the hippo and his water refuge. I remember there were a few such cases in the Manyara area where the deaths were attributed to the hippo. But more are killed by this animal through his attacking fishing canoes, capsizing them, then seizing the helpless victims and biting them in two. Among the herbivore, the hippo has killed more people than any other plant-eating animal, including the buffalo.

There is a constant tug-of-war twixt the hippo and the

fishermen. *Kiboko* (hippo) will destroy their nets, and the fishermen will attempt to spear them whenever convenient. If a hippo is merely wounded, the provoked animal then responds by attacking the fishermen in the canoe. The death toll of human life is thus greater in this manner. I have hunted the *kiboko* in this body of water with its numerous floating islands of bog, many bordered by tall papyrus, giving it a swampy appearance.

On one outing I have along with me my three children and Mervyn, a close friend of mine, with his two young ones. When we arrive, the villagers are overjoyed at the prospects of our eliminating a few of their enemies, but more so, I believe, at the idea of their acquiring some meat in the process. The meat of a *kiboko* is delicious, and the lard rendered from it will not turn rancid. There is no problem obtaining volunteers to paddle the dugouts into the bay where we can hear the hippo.

Gliding between several floating islands, we draw into a large clearing. Immediately we see several hippos. Only their nostrils, eyes, and ears are visible. Nothing much to shoot at! At this distance, aiming at anything below the waterline, the bullet will only glance away and do no harm. We need to be closer so that the angle will cause the bullet to penetrate the water. (I discovered this years ago while hunting muskrats during spring breakup in Saskatchewan.) One by one the hippos sink below the water as we drift toward them, only to appear again some distance away. This is not going to be easy!

They keep bobbing up and down just out of range as we keep drifting around in the bay. We have several hours to spend before dark, so there is no rush. The villagers are collecting along the water's edge. With that crowd fighting over the meat, I had better bring in two or else I may end up with nothing for myself. Indeed, eating is these people's greatest enjoyment! That is why they are waiting patiently out there.

The time comes finally when one *kiboko* lifts his head sufficiently for me to put a bullet in his brain. *Kiboko* rears up out of the water like a submarine and then sinks with a big splash, the water turning red in his wake. He will appear again, belly-up, in ten to twenty minutes. The others do not react much to the whole episode, but keep staring at us, their prominent eyes just level with the water. There must be a dozen or so of them scattered about. I then observe that we are parked right in the hub of the lot! It would be wholly catastrophic should one take a notion to come up under us. We would not stand much of a chance of swimming free of them without mishap.

Our paddler guides the dugout canoe to the edge of the circle of stationed hippos. Noting we are approaching a large island of floating reeds, I shoot my second hippo as we coast by him. I am not overly pleased at his reaction. He sinks quietly. Shortly, we see bubbles of air rising to the surface. Then they begin advancing in a straight line toward us! Frantically we paddle toward the nearby reeds, which I had noticed earlier. Will we make them in time? All our eyes are glued on those air bubbles. The gap between them and our canoe is narrowing rapidly. We brace for the toss! Should have left the kids at home.

The canoe noses into the reeds, and we beach. Where is the hippo? The bubbles just then reach the end of our canoe, half of which is still in the water. The island, ten feet in diameter, though floating, is still large enough to support us and deep enough to prevent the wounded animal from capsizing us. *Kiboko* now surfaces beside us, and I shoot him in the ear. As he sinks there is no doubt that this time he is dead.

We return into the bay and paddle up to the first body, which is now floating. Many of the hippos have retreated farther toward the river, and the remaining few keep their distance. Tying a rope around one leg, we commence towing him. His huge bulk grounds before we can tug him onto the dry land. Then those who are gleefully leaping onshore come

61

into the shallow water and drag the hippo the remaining distance through the muck and mire. There are at least two dozen men present, all shouting and giving commands.

It does not take long before *pangas* are flying, cleaving through the inch-thick hide. There is one who appears to be in charge; at least, his voice carries more volume than anyone else's, including mine. I cannot make myself be heard! I motion that the two hind legs are for me. They nod and I take it they understand. But it ends with me struggling to obtain even one of them! And then I have to guard it constantly after that.

By the time the first carcass is stripped of every morsel, the second hippo has risen and is floating. We return for it, and the process of bringing in the dead animal is repeated. We settle for a front leg this time. Loading our meat, we then drive off, leaving the villagers to divide the second carcass among themselves. We keep hearing their shouting and clamoring for some time as we motor toward home. We are glad to get away from all that hubbub!

*   *   *

Another hunt for hippos is at the same locale. Instead of motoring around on the road and then through a partial forest, I arrange for a canoe to take the whole family and Gary, a young chap, across Lake Manyara. It is a much shorter route and will be a new experience for all of us. The flamingos are there by the thousands as we launch out into the deep. Actually, it is very shallow for some distance, so that we must walk until the canoe can carry us without touching bottom. We enjoy the two-hour safari in spite of the sun blazing down on us all the way.

Marion has come along to take movies of this hunt. Therefore she rides in a second canoe, which stays closer to the shore, away from the hippos and danger. Her paddler knows what he has to do so that she can acquire the best pictures possible. The hippos again number around a dozen, and we have no problem approaching them. I shoot the first one as he lies broadside to us with his head partly showing. He disappears from sight without a sound. Did I really hit him? There was no ricochet.

The hippos are wary now, offering little to shoot at, only their nostrils and eyes protruding. Tired of waiting, I take a bead at one staring directly at me and fire. The bullet skips over his forehead. Too far away for the proper angle. Gary blasts away at one, and the *kiboko* shoots up out of the water, flipping over backward into the bay. He somersaults in this manner several times before settling down to the bottom. During all this commotion and splashing, I shoot at one who has advanced near our canoe and score a direct hit. He sinks in a pool of blood.

A carcass is now sighted floating where I had shot at my first one. It had been a fatal shot after all. There is now going to be sufficient meat for all, should the rest surface. And they do. There is the usual *kelele* (bedlam) when it comes to cutting up the animals after they have been tugged onto dry land. With more meat available for the villagers, we are able to get the portions we want. And I believe it helps to have Marion present on the scene. When she asks for specific cuts, they make sure she gets them.

During Marion's filming, a hippo charged the dugout she was in. When the paddler approached dangerously near the now excited herd, one came for them. The paddler managed to row himself and Marion into shallow waters just ahead of the pursuing *kiboko*. Needless to say, Marion was not using the camera during the flight. Both hands were busy hanging onto the sides of the dugout.

Chapter Nine

Be Careful!

After three hours of tramping through the heavily wooded lowland between Lake Manyara and the escarpment, the scout and I drop in upon a herd of feeding buffalo. Glancing them over, I spy an older male, much heavier than the rest. He is on the near side and carrying a good set of horns. I plant a .458 slug in his rib cage, and the bull sags to the ground. The woods instantly come alive with one-ton brutes milling about. Then the mass stampedes in our direction!

As the wall of bobbing heads closes in on us, I duck behind a large tree and the scout does the same. Over thirty bellowing beasts crash by on both sides. Twigs are snapping all about us. There would not be much left to pick up should we fall under those pounding hooves!

As quickly as it started, it ends. There now remains only a cloud of dust drifting lazily in the wake of the vanishing herd. In front of us, where the air is beginning to clear, lies a gray heap. It is the dead buffalo.

*   *   *

I have hunted these heavyweights in tight cover quite frequently and have exited each time unscathed. Not saying that there weren't times when I wondered if I would. Especially when you happen to be a tagalong. Then your life is dependent on the one in charge of the hunt. Should he be unpredictable, then you may be in for it. The following account is an example. On this occasion, I am escorting a couple of hunters out to Shauri Moyo. This area hugs the escarpment wall and is just south of Lake Manyara, where *nyati* abound in large numbers. It was George, a Greek farmer, who first introduced me to these buff, who literally play hide-and-seek with you in the dense thickets.

We soon find ourselves on foot, deep in thick undergrowth that is interspersed with heavy trees. I trail along with my 30-30, hardly a weapon for hunting buffalo, but I feel safer with it in my hands than without it. I should have brought along the .458, even though it is not my hunt. The 30-30 is in case I meet a bushbuck, for which I have a license.

The woods are crawling with *nyati*. We can hear dry branches breaking as they slide from cover to cover. At times, I catch the movement of leaves closing in behind the retreating herd. As we enter a small clearing, there staring at us from beneath the branches of a stunted acacia stands a buff. He is almost hidden in the shade of the drooping branches, laden with creeping vines. My companion (Mervyn) and I halt with our smaller calibers while the two with their big guns proceed a few more paces.

As the two line up for their shots, the younger of the two squeezes his off first. The black beast answers with an enormous bellow. The older man, who is actually the one in command, does not follow up with his shot, but instead lowers his rifle and is degrading his mate for blowing out his eardrum. "You have blown out my eardrum; you have blown out my eardrum!" he keeps screaming. I am dumbfounded at what is unfolding before me, and so is the buffalo! He does not charge but continues to survey the irate man who is flailing his arms and shouting at his buddy.

Meanwhile, Merv and I are poised on top of a fallen tree, searching for a suitable hiding place should the buff finally charge. But there is no haven for us to dive into or climb onto. Then, to our relief, the bull dashes off and is swallowed up by the green foliage. He was not about to tangle with this colossal human being who could outbellow him. Needless to say, this episode put a kink into the hunt for the rest of the day.

*   *   *

Now mind you it is not a pleasant experience to have a gun explode right next to your head, especially when the weapon is in someone else's hands. This has happened to me three different times. The first time was back in Saskatchewan when I was about twelve years of age. My brother and I had stopped off at our neighbor's farm on our way home from school to play cowboys and outlaws. My school chum and I ended up on the top of their Model A car sitting in the garage. What should be hanging there above the doorway but a shotgun. He pulls it down and sticks it in my face and says, "Stick 'em up!" I grab the end of the barrel and push it aside. Just in time, as the gun is loaded! The bullet blasts a hole through the wall next to my face.

The second time was right here in the Tanganyika bush near Lake Burungi. It is soon after our arrival, and I am out with someone who is after birds. After a fruitless try at several francolin, he returns to the Landrover, which Merv is driving. We do not go far when there is a deafening explosion on my right next to my head. What has happened? Merv, on my left, is afraid to glance our way in case he may discover a couple of headless passengers. I reach for my ear and locate it. It is where it is supposed to be. I then peek to my right. There is a face, drained of all its color, staring straight ahead. "I'm all right," he says. "I've just lost my eardrum." Thank the Lord that is all!

What had happened was that he had neglected to empty the shotgun before climbing into the vehicle. Then instead of holding it between his knees, he stuck it beside his rifle between us. After only a few bumps, the rifle bolt caught the trigger of the shotgun and boom it went off. There was now a neat hole in the Landrover top just next to my head.

The third time was a few years later while after *tembo* in Yaida Valley. There are three of us, besides the tracker and an assistant, marching along in single file on a path which the elephants used only a few hours ago. The wind is in our favor, and at this pace we should catch up to the herd by noon. The man ahead of me has his rifle slung across his shoulder. The barrel is tipped upward, so I'm all right. Mine is cradled in the crook of my arm pointing away and to the sky. It is not cocked, and I believe none of the others are either, as there has not been a need as of yet this morning to fire at anything.

There are times when you can forget to eject the cartridge from the chamber and even, unfortunately, to release the cocked hammer after the antelope you are about to drop suddenly dashes away! Thus far it has not happened to me, but I was with someone when he forgot (besides the one I have just mentioned in the previous account). We had stalked an impala, and when we were within range my companion lined up for a shot. But as he was about to squeeze it off, the animal spotted us and showed us his heels. After tramping back to the Landrover, we climbed up onto it for a look-see. The impala was nowhere in sight. As I was squatting beside the young man, my eyes fell on the rifle in his hands. A cold chill crept up my spine when I discovered the hammer still fully cocked!

Now back on the trail for elephant. As we are crossing an open glade, it happens! There is a powerful blast right behind me. No one is expecting it, least of all me. Stars spin crazily around in my head, but I manage to keep from falling on my face, for I'm caught midstride. Now what happened?

Well, the man bringing up the rear, who is carrying his rifle rather loosely, stumbled on a loose pebble. In the course of regaining his balance, he tightened his grip on the stock, pulling the trigger in the process, not knowing that the safety catch had slipped off sometime earlier. Boom! The slug, which can drop an elephant at one hundred paces, did not miss me by much. Yes, there had been a cartridge left in the chamber.

Ever since then, I do not fancy anyone with a gun directly behind me. I shudder at the thought of it.

*　　*　　*

The person who has gone hunting with me more than anyone else is Mervyn Thomas. Both of us came to Tanganyika at about the same time, and we immediately became buddies. We are more or less interested in the same things. Thus it was that we made numerous hunting safaris together. The first hunt I had in Africa was with Merv. That day I shot a greater kudu, while he got a roan antelope. He accompanied me several times while out after elephants. I remember him always as a gentleman, even when out in the Tanganyika bush.

He and his wife, Sheila, along with their children often came over to spend some days with us. On one of those visits, we decide to have ostrich for our New Year's dinner. With that bright idea, we all climb into our Landcruiser and away we dash in search of one of these birds, everyone out for a nice drive. After all, nothing dangerous about hunting ostrich! Cruising along, Sheila in her Welsh accent comments, "I know something exciting is going to happen, because every time we go out with Stan something unusual takes place."

Numerous ostriches dot the Mbugwe plains, so I turn in

that direction. The white alkaline dust lifts behind the vehicle as we speed over the flats. A few ostriches are spotted standing here and there. In the mirage they appear to be on stilts, their long legs seeming even longer. This first bunch are female, and we are seeking a male. With our glasses we sight one farther on, and we head for him. (The male is black and white, while the female is grayish in color. They are the world's largest birds, standing between seven and eight feet in height.)

Passing a few thorn trees growing in the middle of the flats, we meet a fisherman coming from the lake. Recognizing me, he flags us down. After the customary greetings, he informs me that a buffalo, which has been bothering him and the other fishermen, is now at the lake. The buffalo is an old and mean bull that has been chasing them when they come to inspect their nets. Could I come and shoot him? I watch the others with me for their reactions. I do not want to spoil a peaceful family outing for an ostrich by going after a nasty old buff. They think it is great! Why don't we go and see the buffalo, since he is so near?

We easily locate Nyati. He is lying down not far from the water. Not wishing to disturb him, we stay a short distance away. He is old and quite thin. I did not bring along my big rifle, just the 30-06 and the .22. After all, we were just going for birds! I turn around and we head back to the station, only a couple of miles away, for my .458.

Water is essential to buffalo. Like cattle, they must drink each day. They are also very fond of wallowing in the muddy, shallow pools. When the old bull starts living by himself, he is always found near water. His movements at this time are quite limited. I had the good fortune once before to come upon a lone *nyati* out here on the plains near the waters of Lake Manyara. With my first shot he had plunged into the water, making for the bulrushes a hundred yards away.

On that hunt I had a Msandawi tribesman with me. Being a Bushman, he was excellent as a tracker and skinner. We dashed in after the buffalo with intentions of turning him back to the dry lakebed before shooting again. The water was only knee deep, and we were making better progress than the wounded animal, who, being heavier, sank deeper into the mud. He stopped when we got between him and his destination. We faced each other. All our whooping and arm flapping did not impress him at all. He lunged at us. Thinking he would follow, we made for the shore. He did not accommodate us. Instead, he again made for the bulrushes. I dropped him with my next shot.

Then began the chore of cutting up the animal in the murky water. We could not budge him no matter how hard we tugged. Had he been a wildebeest, we could have managed. I know, as two of us did it once. But it was impossible with this big brute! It was a gory mess by the time we were through. We were covered from top to bottom with mud and you-name-it!

Today, as we are on our way back to the lake, I am praying that this buffalo will not decide to make his last stand in the muddy water as well. We find him as we had left him, still dozing. As we look at him now he does not appear mean at all, just an old animal waiting for the curtain to fall. As we come up behind him, he shows no sign of sensing our presence. Stopping the vehicle at a safe distance, we decide on a plan of action. Merv and I will walk up to him as close as reasonably possible before shooting. Leave enough space for a charge, if there is one, to get in a second shot. Merv is to use the 30-06, which is not going to be easy at close range because of the scope on it. Had intended to use the rifle on the ostrich, which does not allow one too near. Colleen (my daughter) is to climb up on the carrier and take movies of the action, while the rest stay inside the vehicle.

The buffalo is lying with his head lowered, angling away

from us. If he has any knowledge of our presence, he does not show it. We spread apart, Merv going to my left, which puts him right behind the animal. I am fifteen paces from the old beast when I shoot. From the angle I am at, the bullet hits him in the side, but it does not enter the heart. Instead, his hip has deflected the shot. There is instant reaction. The lifeless animal before us is now springing to life!

He thrusts himself erect and spins around all in one motion. For an old bull who was supposed to be sleeping he moves extremely fast. Behind us I hear Sheila shout, "Be careful, Mervyn!" A quick sideways glance shows Merv with his rifle raised, trying to find, in the scope, the right spot on the animal to shoot.

The buffalo is enormous as he covers the distance rapidly between us. He charges straight for me! Then the whole scene kicks into slow motion. He drops to his front knees after our bullets hit him, mine in his chest and Merv's near his eye. The old bull struggles gallantly to raise himself. Lifting his head, he bellows, desperately wanting to cover the remaining few paces to drive his huge horns into me. When the next bullet from the .458 hits him, he sinks slowly, his hind legs buckling under him.

We approach him from the side. To make certain he is out of commission, Merv gives him one more from his rifle. The buffalo jerks. The old bull is defiant to his last breath! My hat goes off to this courageous beast, game to the very end. We later find, when we are cutting him up, my second bullet. It had gone through his heart! He really had wanted to take someone with him.

It had all happened so quickly. None of us dreamt that this much could take place in the space of fifteen seconds. I need to add here that Colleen kept grinding away on the camera during the charge, faithful to the task given her.

What about the ostrich? After we haul home the buffalo,

we resume our hunt for the bird. He is still standing out there waiting for us. I bag him, and we end up having ostrich for our New Year's dinner after all.

Chapter Ten

Solitary Bulls

When an elephant bull ages, he gets crankier and more short-tempered. Soon the frolicking of the young, the constant caring for the herd, and the challenges of leadership from other bulls just get too much for him. Then, either through his own choice or by force, he leaves the herd and starts to live a solitary life. One or two bachelor bulls may go along with him to act as his *askari* (guards). They now inhabit the dark and lonely places in the African bush.

I came across such a bull on one of my safaris. A lone *askari* is watching over him while the old fellow stands dozing. I close in on them as near as I dare without giving myself away. The breath of air is now coming my way, and at any moment the *askari* might notice my movements. Their eyesight is not that keen, but any gesture within sixty-five yards they will detect. I am about that distance now.

The old one is facing me, and the *askari* is angling away. I have with me only a tracker, and he remains behind as I commence to stalk. I know if I hit the old one right, he will fall without knowing what happened. But if I do not, I will have two of them to contend with instead of just one. I shoot and the old bull drops dead on the spot with a bullet in his brain. The *askari* receives the shock of his life! It is a complete surprise to him. Wheeling around, he hurries to the fallen giant, only to discover he is not responding to his nudges. He then sets out to find the one who has done this thing to his chief.

The *askari* charges off in the direction to my right. Going a short distance, he stops and tests the air with his trunk. Coming up with nothing, he returns to the fallen patriarch. He then tries another direction—mine! He rushes all out in a charge. I do not move. I know he has not detected me yet, or else he would have come at me in his first charge. He keeps coming! I am ready to shoot him if I have to, but I do not want to do it. His ivory is not worth it. *Askari* are usually immature bulls, therefore carry small tusks.

He halts less then twenty paces in front of me, his trunk searching for my scent. I hold my breath. He swings around and returns to the dead bull, only to resume rushing off in another direction, this time to my left. He does this in all four directions before concluding that the one who has done this is nowhere near. He lunges off to my right and disappears into the forest. I tarry awhile in case he returns. But he does not.

I walk up to the old elephant. His tusks, though not long, are heavy. Looking around to see where my tracker has gone to, I find him standing exactly where I left him. He has not moved an inch. It is always a great relief to have the tracker or skinner assist you in this manner. I have heard of those who, by making the wrong move, get trampled to death by an irate animal or by a fleeing herd wishing to vacate hurriedly the field of danger. The latter proved almost true in one of my hunts in Tarangire forest.

*   *   *

The tracker and I are alone after this herd. There is a good tusker in there, and we have no problem following their spoor. The tracks made in the morning dew are easy to read. We soon find ourselves in heavy foliage. It is now impossible to see beyond a few yards. A huge python, stretched across several branches, eyes us as we pass within a few feet of him. He has fed recently, for he does not move.

A branch cracks ahead of us! We have overtaken the herd. Let's hope they are still bunched and not spread out too much in this tight bush. I take the lead and continue stalking, only more stealthily now. The trees thin out abruptly, and in the small clearing loom three elephants just ten paces away! I know there are more, as there is movement to my left among the trees. But I am going to have to shoot quickly, as one of the three in view is the one I want, and he is staring right at me.

The gun roars and my bull drops. Immediately the trees off to my left come alive! Six or seven appear and collide with the two ahead of me in their panic. Which direction will they take next? Two turn to face me. I am poised for a charge. Then those still partially hidden from me plunge deeper into the forest and the two before me follow them. I breathe a sigh of relief.

Now where is my tracker? I recall, as I was lining up for my shot, catching a glimpse of someone disappearing into the brush ahead of me and to my left. Why he ducked by me instead of seeking shelter in the growth behind me is beyond me. I call his name. No reply. I call again. Nothing. I walk over to where I had last seen him vanish. Surely he did not get trampled by the milling herd? Were there more elephants unseen by me?

Entering the tree line, I spy him hiding under some brush. He is lying facedown with his hands crossed over the back of his head. No wonder he cannot hear. I nudge him with my toe. He turns slowly and gazes up at me with terror in his eyes. Yes, he is alive and unharmed, a relief to both of us. Had the herd come in my direction he would certainly have been trampled to death. They would not have seen him there, hiding under the brush. Why did he choose to do what he did? I do not know. He cannot tell me either. But it is one of those things that could have cost him his life.

*   *   *

Magola has been spotted now and then by the wandering Watindiga in the rugged mountainous range between Yaida Valley and Lake Eyasi. The fleeting glances the giant, solitary bull offered them, when they intruded his private haunts while searching for wild honey, convinced them that he really did exist. This colossal elephant had tusks so heavy that in order to climb a steep ridge, he had to turn around and back up, dragging along his ivory. Evidence of this happening were common findings. I personally have come across marks left by an elephant dragging his tusks along the ground, but whether they were made by Magola or by another tusker I am not prepared to say.

Each time we started on Magola's trail we ended up, after several days of tracking, bagging another *tembo*. Magola simply would vanish. By crossing the feeding grounds of a large herd, he would lose us when his tracks were obliterated by the milling cows and calves. As each attempt to discover him failed, I came to the conclusion that Magola is but a phantom.

I cannot say that we did not try to dispel my conclusion. We would spend hours glassing the ridges and hidden gorges daily in our search for him. But eventually we would run out of time and give up on this elusive ghost. The countless miles clambering over broken terrain and the chilly nights cramped among the windy crags were of no avail in our quest for Magola. The bugs and mosquitoes that plagued us, the lack of water for drinking and for bathing when the seasonal streams turned up dry, they just added to our frustrations.

*   *   *

The disadvantage of hunting these solitary bulls is their number. They are alone or at times accompanied by an *askari* or two. They are not easily detected when reduced to such a small number. It is much easier to spot a full herd from a knoll. Even when on ground level, they are readily heard while feeding by the snapping and cracking of branches. Their screams bounce back and forth between the hills as they settle family disputes.

After having said this, I wish to add that there is one advantage to hunting solitary bulls. You do not have to contend with an unpredictable herd! It is just you and him with his *askari*. With a herd you have the mama (female) with her *watoto* (young ones) barring your way, should you drop a *dume* (bull) in their midst. And I cannot forget the dreaded tuskless female who charges you at the slightest provocation! Countless times I have had such a one crashing through the undergrowth behind me as I fled for my very life.

On one such occasion, we happen to have along with us Frank, a missionary from Kenya. He brings along Elmer, his friend from the States, who wishes to experience the excitement of an elephant hunt. We are up at four-thirty and on our way. After gulping down breakfast, we decide to try the forest which runs along the brim of the escarpment. Here a solitary bull has been spotted daily for the last while, near Madunga village.

To get to Madunga, we have to leave the road from Dongabesh and take a rugged track leading into the forest. After seventeen miles of grinding, the Landrover stalls. We soon discover that it is jammed in third gear and cannot be pushed backward. The owner of the vehicle sends the two men he brought along to fetch someone with a vehicle from Dongabesh. Meanwhile we continue to work on the vehicle. By two-thirty we realize it is hopeless. It is decided then that Elmer and I walk on to the nearest settlement, a Lutheran

Mission, leaving Frank with Ralph to sleep in the Landrover—should that be necessary.

I must admit that Elmer is taking the grueling walk very well, considering he is not accustomed to it as I am. Only as we are nearing our destination does he require a periodic rest. Finally, we arrive at the station, having covered the seventeen miles in four and a half hours. A kind nurse treats my friend's sore feet, which now have sprouted blisters the size of cherries. We are given a hot meal and then a bed for the night. Yes, the two men who were sent had arrived and a missionary was on his way to the stranded vehicle with his Landrover. Why had we not seen them? They had taken another trail.

This unexpected setback has delayed my return home. No way now to get back there on time to get my children to school in Arusha. Their classes commence in the morning. It rains all night; finally the day breaks. I catch a ride with one of the workers on the station who is traveling to Arusha, and en route we pick up the children. Then at six o'clock in the evening, after a two-hour road delay, Colleen and Kirk are finally dropped off at school.

Meanwhile, our hunt resumes the following day when Jerry in Arusha offers to assist us with his vehicle. By evening we are again in elephant country. Yaida Valley is chosen this time around and not the forest where the breakdown occurred two days ago. It has been raining there ever since, but the weather we encounter here in the valley is fair.

We set up camp in the vicinity of Mono. Klipspringer can be spotted on the hill next to our site. Earlier we had seen zebras in the distance. Lions are roaring nearby as darkness closes in on us within our tent. Then in the middle of the night there is a racket just outside! What is it? Lions? We stiffen out and no one breathes. I grip my rifle, which lies beside me. Will our two guests, Frank and Elmer, who are snugly zipped in their sleeping bags, come to their end out here in the Tanganyika bush?

In the morning light, we discover the tracks of two rhino near the tent, one set only ten feet away from where our heads had been! They must have been the ones who had awakened us. During the day, an impala is bagged for the meat pot. We even come across some roan antelope as we scout for elephant. Finally, toward evening we discover a herd within marching distance. They are congregated near one of the hills.

From the hill we size up the herd and get our bearings. With the breeze in our face we approach the herd. I will not be taking part with my rifle this time. Instead, I wish to take movies of the action. When we are as near to our intended victim as the circumstances will allow, I am ready with my camera. The elephants are unaware of our presence. Through my lens I see the bull take the shot. Then others are flashing across my view. Behind me I hear, above the bedlam, someone shout, "Run, quick!"

Lowering my camera, I see a tuskless cow bearing down on me. Peering through my camera to photograph the stampeding herd, I had failed to see her approaching outside the perimeter of the camera lens. Spinning around, I plunge after the others, who are fleeing for the rocks on the nearby hill. Even if I had a rifle with me instead of my camera, I still would have done the same. Why? The charging *tembo* is not carrying any ivory!

Fortunately, the distance is short and there are huge boulders at the base. We all find cover ahead of the stampeding herd and stay put until they settle down and leave. The cow without tusks is the last one to exit! We find the dead bull right where he had fallen.

*   *   *

On a later date, Jerry and I find ourselves on another hillside in Yaida Valley. We have been on the lookout for a solitary bull elephant who is supposed to be in this area. We want to find out whether his tusks are good enough to bother with him. There is a herd not far away to our right, but it contains mostly cows with their calves. The few bulls that are there are not very old, as their ivory is not that heavy.

We are up high enough to be able to see into the forest stretching out below us. The tracker we have is glassing the landscape with us, and it appears the old bulls are masters at concealing themselves. That is why they get to be old.

It has been hours since we climbed this hill. Surely we will see one of these old monarchs soon. Then our patient vigil is rewarded! First we spot his gray back. It could easily pass for one of the boulders below us. That is where he is, right at the base of our hill! We have been glassing the distant places, not thinking that he would be so near us. He moves a step and stops. Still have not seen his tusks. Should have reasonable ivory, as he is of a good stature.

Though not a hundred yards from us, he makes a poor target. He slips in between the trees, keeping himself well hidden at all times. We are also up too high for a good shot, should one even offer itself. Need to get down lower. We still have not seen how heavy his tusks are. Once in a while we see some ivory gleaming through the branches, but never the length of them.

While we are making our way down the hill, the bull hears us. We see him change direction and head for deeper cover. In spite of being the largest land animal, weighing as much as six tons and standing up to thirteen feet high at the shoulder, an elephant can move silently as a shadow when the need arises.

Stumbling down the rest of the way, we light out after him. We pick up his tracks where we last saw him. They are

A Leopard Outside Our Window

The Giraffe, Marion's Favorite Animal

Colleen with a Spurfowl

A Hare

And a Genet

"Leave my dik-dik alone!"

Lions prowled around our tent that night.

The Puff Adder That Got into My Office

Jo-Jo, the Pet Monkey

"Simba! Simba!"

A Native Hyena Trap

"Don't be afraid, Kirk!"

Chui, the Leopard

A Tommy

One of Marion's Good Shots

An Impala

A Reedbuck

Kirk and Mark with a Beautiful Pair

Each Tusk Weighing over 100 Pounds!

Colleen with a Cobra

Kirk with a Catfish from Our River

A Ten-foot Mamba

The Hippo Who Came after Our Boat

Hippo Hunting on Lake Manyara

One of Those Bagged and Tugged to Shore

Following in Dad's tracks, Colleen and Kirk—

both crack-shots!

big. And he is alone. He is running straight into the wind. After a half of a mile of this, he veers sharply to his left. He is now trying to get the wind in his favor. That way he will know our whereabouts each step of the way! We can tell he is a wise one.

We converge abruptly upon his hiding place. He is not around, but there is plenty of spoor. We know that he knows we are on his trail by all the signs he has left behind. Once before when in pursuit of a small herd, which we had spooked, it was quite easy to keep on their trail due to what the chase did to their nervous system. They left plenty of signs in their wake.

We are able to tell why he gave up the ambush. We had come up to him on his flank. He had miscalculated. Instead of moving along slowly as he thought we would do, we had rushed headlong and stuck closer to him than he had figured. Thus we came up to him in a direction he was unprepared for. Upon hearing us, he resumes his flight, keeping the breeze in his favor.

We are winded from the hard run we have made. This allows the bull to gain on us considerably. We stick to his trail. Then we come up to another station where he had stood watching his backtrail. By the signs he has left behind, he had been waiting for some time. The question now is should we keep after him. The next time he may be successful in his attempt to bushwhack us! And where were his *askari*? He may be on his way to where he has left them, leading us into another kind of an ambush.

With this in mind, we give up the chase and return to where we left the tracker—at the base of the hill.

Chapter Eleven

Ever on the Alert

One has to tread lightly and be ever on the alert for snakes, as they are plentiful where we resided in the Tanganyika bush. The puff adder in his brown and black suit is hard to spot when walking along through the grass. While stalking a herd of elephants, I was about to place my foot down when I spotted him! A puff adder lying beside the trail we were using. He must have been waiting for some prey to pass by in front of him. He was poised and ready to strike when I brought the hunting ax down on him.

They camouflage so well into their surroundings. Any carelessness on your part can shorten your life unexpectedly. They are slow movers and catch their prey by lying as if asleep or dead. It is not difficult then to step on one when failing to be fully alert in bushy territory. His length of only four feet can easily be overlooked. He kills more people in Africa than any other snake.

A puff adder crawls into our house via my office door, which stands ajar most of the time due to the heat. The snake then chooses to lie in front of the bookshelf. How long he has been there I do not know, but when I bend over to pull out a book, my mind registers something out of the ordinary. At the bottom of my range of vision are strips against the tan floor. Glancing down, I see the puff adder lying motionless, only inches from the end of my boot! Leaning backward cautiously, I reach for the *rungu* (club of the Masai) standing in the corner. With it the snake is dispatched quickly. Had I failed to spot him in time, the result of his bite would have been death in less than twenty-four hours due to hemorrhaging of the mucous membranes.

A relative to the puff adder is the night adder. They are not as readily seen owing to their nocturnal way of life. Bites by them are usually gotten when walking about at night. The venom is less toxic to man than that of their daytime cousins, and the night adders reach a length of just three feet. Had it not been for the torch I was carrying I may have stepped on one and been bitten by him one night. The light revealed the night adder lying alongside our well just inches from my boot!

*　　*　　*

Pythons are numerous in the vicinity. There are the species which are found on land and then the ones which reside in the water. Many of the latter are caught by villagers annually in fish traps, as their diet consists of sea life. They can get as long as ten feet, while their land cousin can reach the grand length of thirty feet!

This large python, after devouring a gazelle, will slither up a tall acacia tree. There he snoozes on top of the branches for days until the animal inside is digested. When the pangs of hunger again grip him, he glides back to earth and resumes his hunt. He coils around his prey, slowly suffocating it to death, then commences to swallow it. After this is accomplished, it is up the tree for him once more.

Due to their dormant life, not many are readily seen. A python slipped unannounced under the table-saw for some shade during a dinner break one day. When we returned to resume our work, he startled us by rearing up. Grabbing up one of the two-by-fours lying at my feet, I managed to dispose him after a few misses, as he turned out to be quite agile.

*   *   *

I find the cobra more of an adversary than the puff adder or the python. Whereas the puff adder depends entirely on his bite to procure his meal, the cobra has another weapon, which he uses effectively when not in range to strike. He is able to spit venom accurately from as far away as fifteen feet. Many a victim is blinded before the cobra sinks his fangs into his prey. His poison affects the nervous system, causing paralysis and finally death in a comparatively short time. This snake is glossy black with a speckled throat, which spreads out resembling a hood when he is ready to spit venom into your eyes. Thus the name spitting cobra. He can reach ten feet in length.

You can expect to find the cobra anywhere. But for the sunglasses I was wearing, I would have received the venom in my eyes and been blinded on one occasion. While I was counting mud blocks one forenoon, he struck from his hiding place in between one of the rows stacked next to where the men were making mortar. Never did get the cobra. Too well hidden. They are masters at it.

One of the places they choose to make their homes is the vacated termite mounds. When you spy their deadly enemy, a mongoose, tarrying on top of one of these huge anthills, you can be sure there is a family of cobras inside. When we were hacking out our station in the bush, many termite mounds had to be removed. (Their soil makes good mud blocks.) Cobra nests were found in most of them, containing young ones or unhatched eggs.

They were so numerous around the place that for the first several years it was not uncommon to see one or more

94

almost daily. We had to keep the grass in the compound cut short. Marion, snipping grass around the foundation of our house one morning, was startled to see the head of a cobra pop up in front of her. I ran over to her when I heard the scream. She was shaken up badly! But the damage had been done. There lay the snake minus his head! The cobra had chosen to rear up just as Marion was closing the shears. The momentum of the swing carried through in spite of her being spellbound. She was surprised to see him dead.

Two workers on our station were bitten by a cobra, and both narrowly survived. One, a house girl, coming to start work in the morning stepped on the doormat before entering the house. Under it a cobra happened to be snuggled. It struck her on the foot. The second one, a man, was rethatching the wall of his kitchen when he was bitten on his hand by a well-concealed cobra. The bite of one is almost always fatal.

Sitting around in our living room one evening, we are informing our company that they need to be careful when using our outdoor latrine. Before entering it, they must bang the walls, as cobras have been encountered inside on several occasions. I relate the incident where one day as I started to reach for the roll on its shelf, a snake slips out and disappears below. Needless to say, for some time after that my subsequent trips were hurried, with no dillydallying around. On another occasion, one vanished down the hole when I entered and caught him relaxing on the seat. Yes, do not forget to bang on the door!

Before it gets dark, one lady says she needs to make a trip to the outhouse and would her husband kindly accompany her. As he is following her through our living room door onto the veranda, we hear a high-pitched scream and see both barging back inside. "Snake! Snake! There's a snake out there!" I scoot over to the kitchen door and come face to face with a huge cobra under the table on the veranda. He is partly raised and his hood is erect; he is ready to let fly his venom at me. I slash out with the broom I had picked up on my way through the kitchen and catch the cobra as he is drawing back to spit. He measures seven feet and is ebony. The company need an escort after this. They are thoroughly shaken!

*   *   *

A snake more frightening to me than the puff adder, python, or cobra is the black mamba. He is so swift that when he is startled, you see him and then you don't. Though shy, he can be aggressive and very dangerous! His poison is one of the deadliest. His grayish color makes him the most difficult to spot. His cousin, the green mamba, spends most of his time in the trees. On occasions he does enter dwellings. One had to finally be killed when he landed on top of the bed in our girls' quarters, frightening them half to death.

The green mambas love to stretch out on our pickup, which stands in the shade of flamboyant trees near our house. Often I have come upon them resting on the tailgate or on the tires. Without thinking, I enter the vehicle one day and get ready to start the motor. I notice in the corner of my eye a green mamba reposing on the back of the seat. I duck out in a hurry as the snake melts away behind the seat. Before resuming my intentions to drive, I investigate the inside of the cab thoroughly. The green mamba cannot be found. Driving down the road, I cannot help glancing over my shoulder and down on the floor boards every so often. Any moment I expect him to peek up at me from below or from beside me!

The black mamba is much larger than the green mamba, growing up to ten or twelve feet in length. One lazy, hot afternoon as I am lifting up the hood on the Bedford truck, I hear a hissing noise. Looking closely, I see the eyes of a black mamba staring back at me from beneath the engine. He does not act frightened, only keeps making loud hissing sounds at me. Peering underneath the vehicle, I see part of his body. He is draped around the drive shaft. He is a big one! Fetching the .22 rifle, I aim for the part that is hanging loosely from the chassis. After several shots, the black mamba drops down to the ground; here I am able to finish the job. He measures ten feet in length.

One black mamba, also a ten-footer, was fond of lying on top of our outdoor water heater, which stands beside our bedroom. Our worker mentioned to me several times about the snake leaving the place when he approaches to start the fire. Then one morning, upon awakening, Marion and I catch a glimpse of him. Dawn is just breaking and the worker has not yet arrived. The snake is slithering onto the window, which is open. But for the mosquito screens he might have glided inside. Then against the approaching light we see him halt, part of him on top of the ajar metal window.

I sneak from the bedroom and then out of the house. Coming around, I spot him still perched there. The long-handled broom I brought with me catches him as he commences his exit. It strikes the part which is passing over the metal frame. Had the snake been shorter, he would have gotten away, as he was in full retreat.

When the worker is on leave, I am the one to get up in the morning at daybreak to fill the drum with water, stick in the *kuni* (firewood), and light the fire. By the time the rest get up, there is hot water. We have two one-thousand-gallon tanks behind the house which catch the rainwater. From these tanks, during the rainy season, we siphon water into the heater. This one morning, when I was about ready to stick the end of the hose into my mouth to suck up the water, the head of a mamba appears in the opening! Quickly I slap the hose against the building, dislodging him. I could not help thinking of what might have happened had he not revealed himself just then!

I need to mention at this stage that during the fifteen years at Kaiti, not one member of the family was ever bitten by a snake even though they were so numerous on and around the compound. The three children grew up aware of the real dangers that lurked about them and were ever on the alert.

Sitting on the doorstep of our laundry room tinkering with Mark's butterfly net, I hear birds making a big fuss. Glancing up, I see several black weavers flying around nearby. They are excited about something! Soon they are not far from where I am seated. Turning to watch them more closely, I notice they are concentrating on something on the ground. They flutter about and continue their chattering. Then I see the object of their excitement. It is a snake, a big black mamba!

Whether he knows of my presence I am unable to tell. The birds are attracting most of his attention. But I do notice that he is heading in my direction. He is now less than ten feet away! The pole to my son's butterfly net is lying at my feet. Snatching it up, I rise to meet him. The snake sees me and rears up to nearly half his length. I am taken aback! I did not expect this. He is not going to turn and run.

I take a swing at him with the pole. Missed! The mamba moved back in time. I swing again. The same thing happens, only this time he follows up by lunging at me with his upper half. I leap back just in time. After several exchanges with neither scoring a hit, he makes an attempt to retreat, but still fully alert to do damage if he can. One of my swings finally connects. It hurts him, but it does not kill him. He then rises up to my height, reaches way back to avoid my swing, and then lunges at me when I miss.

Instead of pulling back to wind up again for another attempt, I reverse my swing and catch the mamba unexpectedly. A few more whacks and the ten-footer lies dead at my feet.

The black weavers return to their nests. The danger is over.

While climbing one of the local pyramidal hills after the elusive klipspringer, I come to a steep incline. Hanging the rifle around my neck so it rests on my back, I commence working my way up using both hands on the jagged rocks. There is an overhang above me. Be a good place to rest awhile, after I get on top of it.

I am just able to grab the top of the ledge and start to pull myself up onto the overhang. As my eyes come past the shelf, I spy a huge black mamba sunning on the rock not three feet away. I freeze.

He could have struck me then and there full in the face. He had me dead to rights. I was at his mercy. Far from home, I would not have survived. His venom paralyzes the breathing, and I would have expired in less than half an hour. But instead of striking, he chooses to slip away into the crags. That was close! Why had I been so careless? I am supposed to be ever on the alert!

Chapter Twelve

Good Shots

Looking at my trophies, I recall with satisfaction the excellent shots I made when acquiring some of them. There was, for instance, the lone oryx standing under an acacia tree, three hundred yards away, who dropped with my first shot. I had gone out for one that morning and spotted him almost immediately. It was all over as soon as the hunt began. I am quite jubilant as I head on back home. The shot had been made with my 30-30, which does not carry a scope.

Then there was the big bull eland, surrounded by a rather large herd, which was feeding near a dry riverbed. Leaving the children in the vehicle, I scoot down the bank and then sprint along the stream bottom heading in the direction where the antelope are congregated. Trees border the rim above me on both sides. The eland do not detect my presence, nor am I able to see them.

Am I near enough to them now? I cannot reveal my whereabouts too quickly. I may not get another opportunity to approach them this closely again. Should they stampede, they surely will make for an area away from me. I work my way up the bank, careful not to step on any dry twig, for the eland can be wary.

Peeking up over the edge of the riverbed, I sight them directly in front of me. They are no more than a hundred paces away. The eland I want is there in the middle of the herd. You cannot miss him! He is lighter in color, almost gray, and is much taller, by about a foot. He is also carrying a good set of horns.

The only way I am going to get that trophy is to hit his spine above his front shoulders. That is the only spot visible to me from where I am crouched. The head I do not want damaged. Can I make that shot? I must! Carefully I draw a bead. Not much to shoot at. Steadily I squeeze off the shot, and the bull drops from sight. I did it!

I then behold a sight which must be seen to be believed, eland everywhere, leaping over each other! Not as gracefully as the much smaller impala, yet they are able to accomplish this feat just as well when alarmed. Quite incredible for an animal weighing close to a ton. Dust fills the air as the herd heads off into the distance. I return for the vehicle, and the children know by the pleased look on my face that I have bagged my trophy.

The wildebeests have always been plentiful, and numerous good shots have been made during my years of hunting them. They are spunky and have surprised me on several occasions with the courage they possess. The Wambugwe, who hunt them for meat when they have failed to acquire a zebra (their first choice), would tell me to give the wildebeest, when he is alone, wide berth. He can be as dangerous as an old buffalo. He will charge should you approach him too closely on foot.

In a hunt for one of these animals, after I drop him and slit his throat, he surprises us by standing up and charging. Colleen and Kirk, who are with me, clamber up the side of the jeep like monkeys up an acacia tree. I dash to the side of the vehicle where my rifle is leaning. The bull hits the endgate full tilt, blood streaming from his cut throat. He then stands, dazed and confused. The bullet from my gun puts him down for the second time. He does not get up again.

While out for klipspringer on one of our hills, I often glimpsed mountain reedbuck feeding among the boulders. After picking up a license for one, I fail to see them again. Finally, it comes down to the last day. I need to find one today; tomorrow will be too late.

Skirting the brow of the hill, I glimpse two of them making their way through some brush just below me. But they spot me as well and disappear from sight. Am I going to lose them? I wait awhile. Then they reappear. They have worked their way around to where they are now above me. It is quite steep there, which forces them to slow down as they continue their way farther up the sheer wall. I have got to take a shot immediately, before they climb too far.

The buck falls when my bullet hits him, and he tumbles a short distance before coming to rest against an outcrop ahead of me. By the time I have brought my prize down to the vehicle waiting at the bottom, I have slid a hole through the backside of my khaki pants.

Gerenuk are shy animals, inhabiting the dry, brushy scrubland where no water is found for miles. They feed on the scarce green vegetation. They will reach for juicy tidbits as far as they are able while standing erect on their hind legs and craning their abnormally long necks. The natives call them *swala-twiga* (gazelle-giraffe).

I accept the challenge to go on a hunt for one of these seldom seen creatures with my friend Jerry from Arusha. After an hour, we turn off the road which leads to Longido and strike off into the brushland. When a buck with a fine set of horns is finally sighted, I light out after him on foot. He is more vigilant than his cousin the impala, and he soon loses me. But I am determined to make the most of this hunt and continue to search his whereabouts.

How far I have wandered off into this wasteland I am unable to gauge. For the past hour the scenery about me has not changed. Just more and more of the same. There is no breeze, and the sun is a scorcher. I have quit perspiring quite some time ago. In my haste, I left the canteen back in the vehicle.

I detect a slight movement on the far side of the dry bush ahead of me, to my right. I keep walking, not letting on I have noticed the buck's presence. When I am broadside, I catch a glimpse of him from the corner of my eye—twelve paces away. He is the one I want. I veer gradually to my left, and soon the buck is behind me. There are several stunted trees in front of me, and I pass around them. When I feel I am sufficiently hidden from his view, I duck down and peer back to see if he is still standing there.

I am relieved when I see that the buck has not moved. He is not watching me, but is concentrating his gaze on my back-trail. I do not waste another moment. When I have the sight fixed on his right shoulder I squeeze back the trigger. It is not long after when Jerry appears with the Landrover. He had heard the shot. I am satisfied with my trophy.

Zebra hunts usually ended swiftly, as they would be discovered almost immediately and a stallion would drop with my first shot. Nothing much to remember when it is over this quickly, except maybe the excellent shot. I recall one especially that I made with my 30-30 after a short hike through a stand of scorched wait-a-bit thorn bushes, into which my quarry blended perfectly. I spot the stallion eying me from behind some brush, at least three hundred yards away. His head is just visible above it.

I know I will not be able to approach him any closer, as he now knows I have seen him. My 30-06 carries a scope, but it is back at the house. I prefer the 30-30 when on foot in tight bush, as it is easier to handle and lighter to carry because of no scope. I take the long shot, and he drops dead.

A zebra hunt which sticks out in my mind above all the

rest is one that took a lot of elbow and knee grease or, to put it more accurately, elbow and knee skin. This safari finds me in an area north of Mto wa Mbu, a row of *dukas* (shops) sprawled next to a river at the base of the Rift Wall. The place is noted for mosquitoes; therefore the village is appropriately named in Swahili the River of Mosquitoes.

Should you choose to travel north from Mto wa Mbu along a track, you would eventually arrive at Endaruka, where there are ruins of a long-ago civilization. We as a family camped there one night. We inspected the mounds of neatly arranged stones the following day, before jolting our way on to Ol Doinyo Lengai, the Masai's Mountain of God. It is still an active volcano, discharging lava and ashes approximately every six years.

I find the zebras abnormally skittish in this hunting area north of Mto wa Mbu. I am unable to approach them openly. This is probably due to the poachers operating from out of the nearby trading center. Only one choice left and that is to crawl up to them on my hands and knees, as there is no cover besides what the dry grass (which is no taller than two feet) offers. I leave Kirk at the vehicle and commence my stalk.

The ground is level and covered with pebbles that grind into my elbows and knees as I pull myself along. I halt now and then to peer over the grass. Yes, they are still feeding out there, but yet too far away for a decent shot. I continue my stalking in this unusual pose. Sweat is rolling down the bridge of my nose. Then a frightening thought hits me, which causes me to perspire even more! What if I should suddenly come face to face with a snake?

Only recently, this very thing actually happened to a hunter lying in the grass eying the animal he was preparing to shoot, when a cobra raised himself to peer at him—only ten feet away! Fortunately for him, he had a companion close by, who shot the snake before he could spit out his venom into the eyes of the now helpless hunter.

No one nearby to come to *my* assistance should I be confronted by a similar snake. Perspiration is soaking my shirt. My knees and elbows are getting raw from wriggling along on my stomach over the loose pebbles. For an hour I work at it, until finally I am two hundred yards from them. Dare not use up any more time, as it is already six o'clock. Several zebras have started to head out, most likely for water at the river.

Allowing myself a few more moments to catch my breath and for the muscles to quit quivering, I rise up on my knees. Their sentinel will surely spot me, but I hope to get the shot off before he signals an alarm. A sentinel is always posted when they feed in tall grass, as lions stalk them in a similar fashion as I just did.

My gun booms and the stallion, who is about to gallop off, hits the dust. I shakily get up, and after verifying that he is dead, I head back for my vehicle, some distance away. Kirk helps me skin the animal and cut up the meat, as it is too heavy for us to load onto the vehicle. We return home in the dark.

Before I close off this chapter I want to add one more incident that I feel merits an entry. It was not only good shooting, but it was more than I asked for.

We are in need of some meat at the station, so taking some men with me, I head out across the Great North Road for a hartebeest. These antelope do not stray far from the light bush which is scattered alongside the Tarangire forest. Their meat is excellent, beaten in taste only by that of the eland. Actually, the most tender steaks I have eaten off any wild game are those from the reedbuck! I put their meat at the head of my list. The family and I preferred game meat over local beef because it was much more tender and, of course, it contained no insecticide.

I do not travel far before I spot five *kongoni* (hartebeests) all grouped in belly-deep grass. They stare at us as we approach them in a straight line. Their very long, narrow heads and sloping backs give then a clumsy appearance. As soon as they show signs of abandoning us, I halt and send a bullet from my 30-06 at one of the males. (Both the female and the male have horns which are doubly curved.) They bounce away in their peculiar gait that is so different from that of any other antelope. After a short distance, they stop and gawk at us again. I move toward them cautiously. Still cannot believe it that I missed my first shot back there.

I am now in position once more and squeeze back the trigger when the sights of the rifle come to rest on the chest of the one standing broadside to me. The *kongoni* disappears into the tall grass. I make my way to the spot and discover not one animal but two of them! They are both dead. The bullet has passed through the one I aimed at and then entered a second *kongoni*, which was standing exactly beside him, only on the far side from me. Their stance had been such that they appeared to me as being just one animal!

It is not too uncommon for a hunter to drop two animals with one shot. I have done it before with zebra. At that time I had actually seen the second animal standing not far from the one I was planning to shoot. Did not dream, though, that the bullet would pass on through the stallion and still have enough velocity to drop another zebra beyond him. It is always comforting to know that your license allows you to take more than one of most species of game.

After loading the two *kongoni* onto the jeep, we wend our way homeward, passing the spot where I had first sighted them. What should greet me there but another animal lying dead, almost hidden in the tall grass! It is the first *kongoni* I had fired at. I did hit him then! Got more than I asked for.

Chapter Thirteen

Bad Eyes

In hunting you have your good days and your bad days. You never know when you will come up with the latter. If you did, then you would know when to stay home. Save yourself the trouble of going out there in the hot sun, jolting across the rough terrain miles without end, and then stalking your animal that keeps eluding you no matter how determined you are or what you try. It is wonderful what hunting can do right about then for your sore feet!

Hunting is strenuous. You must be physically fit, for often you will find yourself walking for miles, up and down hills, stalking your game in a doubled up position with your chin on your knees or inching along on your stomach over stony ground. You bathe in the cold woodland streams or in the rocky pools and drink from waters alongside the massive footprints and dung heaps of the ever present elephant. Hunting demands a strong heart, a sharp eye, and quick reflexes. You return home after a few days not only tanned and rugged, but renewed and ready to take on the work you have come to do.

I am a lover of the wilds. I love the bush and the savanna with all its animals and birds. I like to be among them and will not kill them needlessly. It is here, more than anywhere else, that I have witnessed the dawn ushered in by songsters appearing on every tree. Then after sunset as the camp fire casts deep shadows around me, far off I hear the yelp of the jackal and the melancholy howl of the wandering hyena. Nearby in the bushes there are a variety of noises. I would not want it any other way.

We are out of meat, and it is decided we get a Tommy and a wildebeest. I have room for them on my license. The old Bedford is handy today, so we take it. Several workers clamber on the back to help with the loading; then we take off. Marion is with me. Not often does she accompany me on my hunting safaris. Finds it too rough on her. But because we are hunting on the old lake bottom of Mbugwe flats, where it is level, she willingly comes along. It is a good thing she does.

Vast herds of wildebeests are always seen traversing our side of Lake Manyara. That is, except today. We drive for miles without spotting one. What has taken place? Even during migration season some always stay behind, reluctant to leave the confines of this valley. We drive as far as the controlled area. We cannot go farther. Ahead of us we see in the shimmering heat waves wildebeests. The rascals. We turn around and head back to where we had seen Thomson gazelles.

The Tommy, as he is better known, lives out on the open plains. Never found in deep cover. Hunting them is quite an easy matter. They will let you approach them to within two hundred yards. Any closer and they are liable to dash away. After darting from you a hundred yards or more, they stop, their short tails twitching back and forth. This is repeated for as long as you fail to get your Tommy. If you keep after them, they lead you back to your starting point. They have led you in a complete circle. If it is a buck you are stalking, he wants to return to his harem. If it is a mixed group, then a doe is anxious to return to her hidden young.

Well, try as I may, I cannot hit my buck! Around and around we go. I empty my 30-30—that is, seven bullets—and

I have not even scratched him once! It is getting to be embarrassing. The fellows in the back of the lorry and my wife in the cab are all looking at the mighty hunter who cannot even hit an animal broadside one hundred yards away. What gives?

I load my Winchester again. I have got to get him, to save face. I am completely shaken by now. The sight is off; that is for sure. But which way? The only targets in this vast emptiness are the Tommies. So I keep guessing. The wisp of alkaline dust where the bullet strikes only tells me I have missed again. Then my rifle is empty for the second time.

I remember the first time I took out my 30-30 on a hunt. We had been in Tanganyika only a few months when I found myself in the bush with my rifle in hand, approaching a herd of wildebeests resting in the shade of some acacia trees next to Lake Burungi. I was alone. The others were after birds. I had a box of twenty shells in my pocket.

Kept approaching them until they began to fidget and show signs of removing themselves from the vicinity. I brace the gun against the tree and fire. Nothing happens. They turn to look at me. I fire once more. Nothing again. I was not even coming close to the big black bull I was aiming at! After I empty the rifle twice, there still is no sign of a hit!

By now I know it is shooting high, as no dust has been kicking up between the beast and me. My sixteenth slug knocks a branch off the tree the bull is under. Wow! Am I ever shooting high! At least eight feet! I have only four rounds left to get my animal. Need to do some accurate calculating right now to narrow down the odds.

The herd is milling about. The shooting has made them nervous. I miss my next shot. It must have been close, as the herd starts to pull out. They must have heard the whine of the bullet. The bull has not moved. He is staring back at me, daring me to hit him. I do not with my eighteenth bullet.

This is getting to be ridiculous! The animal is standing

over yonder, yet I am sighting at the ground midway between him and me. I drop still lower with my next aim and pull the trigger. It is my next to last shot. The wildebeest drops as if clubbed. The bullet just caught his backbone. I run over and finish him off with my last slug. The herd stops a short distance away. Then they commence returning to where I am, sitting on the dead wildebeest. I wave my arms at them, and they halt only a few yards away. They form a half circle and stare blankly at me. I am out of bullets, so we just have to wait each other out. The stalemate is broken when the vehicle returns with my two companions.

Now here I am in a similar situation once more. The same rifle is way off! The only difference between the two target practices is that I had no spectators the first time! I hear the workers talking amongst themselves: *"Macho mabaya"* ("Bad eyes"). They do not realize that it is the rifle's fault and not my eyes! But as far as they are concerned, it is my eyes. *"Macho mabaya,"* I hear them say again.

I'll show them all. I pick up the .22 rifle, which is with Marion. A hit in the head will put him down easily. This time I pick on a new buck. I pull the trigger and miss! The gazelle darts away. A few more shots and they are all misses. It is unbelievable! "Oh, it's Bwana's eyes; they're bad today," the workers are mumbling.

Marion cannot stand it any longer and says, "Let me try a shot!" *And why not?* I thought. She has probably been saying to herself for some time, *Surely I can do better than that!* I hand her the rifle. After a few misses she will be satisfied. And so will those guys on back of the lorry. They will find out that it is not my eyes, but the guns.

The gazelles are restless and will not stand still. So she takes a shot at the running buck. She is really making sure that she will miss. But she does not! The Tommy drops dead with a bullet in his head.

Well, all the way home the men in the back are singing a new song, all about the mama with the *kali* (sharp) eyes. What about me? Anything that I could say would only make things worse. So I just say it to myself and keep the vehicle heading homeward. Today's incident will be repeated for a long time to come. It happened to be one of my bad days!

Just in case you are thinking that it was a fluke how Marion downed the running Tommy with a brain shot, I want to add that she is very accurate with the small rifle. Often we have competed to see who could drop the most sausage-shaped fruit from the tree behind the guest house. Our aim was to nick the stem, and the weight of these huge sausages would do the rest. She usually won the meets we had, often downing twice as many as I did.

Chapter Fourteen

Lost

There are vast areas of *nyika* (wilderness) in Tanganyika wherein one can easily get lost if he becomes negligent at watching his trail for signs (especially his backtrail). When I was still new in the territory, I would take someone along to guide me back out safely. But often I would go at it alone, a stretch at a time, until I had a mental map of the area. This helped me many times to find my way back when out on a hunt deep in the *nyika*.

It is a strange feeling to find yourself suddenly disoriented! I have had this happen to me a couple of times. This was during the time I still had not gotten familiar with my *nyika*. There is a miniforest of palm trees between the Great North Road and Lake Manyara. Interspersed throughout is tall coarse grass and thorny brush. This makes it unpleasant to walk after game at any time, unless maybe after a good fire. The tsetse fly dwells here, the fly so notorious for the spread of sleeping sickness, which is fatal to man and his livestock. Thus this *nyika* is a haven for wildlife.

The Masai herd their cattle along the lake and in this forest. One evening a rhino charges a herd and stampedes them into the palm forest. In trying to retrieve them, the herd boy eventually gets hopelessly lost when darkness falls. The elders show up at midnight to report the incident to us. The cattle had returned to the *boma* as always at dusk, but not the boy. I promise to join them in the hunt early in the morning. In a few hours we find him, bitten up from mosquitoes but alive. Fortunately, a lion or hyena had not found him before we did! The boy just happens to be the son of the village chief. The end of the matter is the father makes me his blood brother after an exchange of gifts.

A grassy marsh lies between the palm forest and the station—all the way to the lake. During the rains, I am unable to pass through here with the vehicle to hunt the wildebeests, zebras, or gazelles that gather near the water. In order to get there, I have to go around—another direction, which is several miles farther. As the short route is only a couple of miles, I often walk it, taking along with me one or two men to help bring back the meat. When the animal is only a reed-buck, impala, or gazelle, we have no problem. But when a wildebeest is shot, it takes a lot of stamina to carry all the meat back home.

On one of these treks to the lake I do not allow myself sufficient time for the round-trip. Did not get the wildebeest as quickly as I had planned. It has rained recently and the alkaline flats are greasy. We slip around while stalking the skittish herd for some time, when finally I drop one as near as possible to the edge of the marsh. The sun slides behind the escarpment just as we finish cutting up the animal. It is dissected so that the hindquarters can be hung around the neck, resting on the carrier's shoulders. This task goes to the tallest and strongest man, by the name of Tembo Saba, which means Seven Elephants in Swahili. The name suits him. The second man and I end up carrying a front quarter each. We set out for home well after dark.

The two men wish to take the path back which leads around the marsh, while I choose the shortest route back—through the marsh. It is the way we had come. I want to get home as quickly as possible. When we had come, we had followed no path, as there wasn't any. You just strike out and choose your own way through the tall grass and around the outcrops of trees.

Soon I can no longer see the distant hills against the skyline, no matter how low I crouch. It just is too dark. The three pyramidal hills a mile from the station should now be on the far side. But they no longer are visible. I try to keep my course as straight as possible. Soon I realize that by rounding another palmetto, avoiding a baobab tree here and a thorn tree there, I surely am fooling myself if I believe that I am still pointing in the right direction!

Then, ringing through the night air, comes a long drawn out howl from a prowling hyena! He has caught the scent of the meat I am carrying. Soon there will be others! I must hurry. I have my rifle, but in the pitch darkness I cannot see far. I keep telling myself, *Now don't get frightened.* I remember someone telling me that lions can smell fear in man and soon follow him. I remember and try. I know if I veer a little to the left, I will miss the station and carry on until I hit the Great North Road. This means walking back a mile. I conclude that if I miss, it would be better to be more to my right. In that direction, I will hit the riverbed, which will then lead me to the station. The Tarangire River runs by our station and empties, when there is plenty of rain, into Lake Manyara. Right now, it is dry.

As I stumble along, any object blacker than the night takes on the form of a hyena or a lion (which happen to be quite numerous in the area). I have heard both on countless nights before retiring. While somewhat shy during the day, they can be extremely bold at night. I circle wide of the baobab trees, not giving a waiting hyena or lion any easy prey. I also think of the leopard, who may be watching me right now from one of the branches! Startled nightjars strain my nerves

114

still further, as they fly up from under my feet.

When I hit the riverbed, it is only a short distance to the station. I can see the light faintly through the trees which surround the compound. I have calculated quite accurately. It is time I did arrive home, for a hyena just across the riverbed answers the one following me. What about the two men with the rest of the meat? They trot in a short time later. We all have safely brought home our loads. The following day I feel the aches in my shoulders, but I am thankful to be in one piece.

*　　*　　*

Much has been said about the natives not getting lost. But I have seen them just as lost as I was one night in the Tarangire forest! I had gone out hunting some meat for the pot and taken two men with me to help load the animal onto the vehicle. Several hartebeests were recently seen just across the road—so that is the direction we take.

I drive for an hour and cannot see a single *kongoni*. They do not like the dense thickets or forest, instead prefer the open country and light bushland or savanna. They are usually seen in small herds with one or two posed on a termite mound as a scout, ready to give warning of any immediate danger. None can be spotted on these perches. With the day wearing on, I decide to venture farther in beyond the tree line. They may have wandered in deeper for reasons unknown to us.

Eventually we come across a herd of zebras and search the vicinity, as *kongoni* often associate with zebras. There just are not any to be found! Only one thing left to do now, as it is getting late, and that is to shoot a zebra. We need meat. This I do and when it comes to loading him onto the vehicle, we cannot manage! (A zebra can weigh as much as seven hundred pounds and stands over four feet at the shoulder.)

I see we are wasting time trying to load the animal and decide to dash back to the station to fetch more help. Since I will be returning with more men, I drop another zebra. This will assure us of enough meat for all the workers. When told to stay behind with the fallen animals, the two men refuse, saying that they are afraid of the lions who will now be on the prowl. They climb in and I take the shortest route possible back home.

After loading up four more men, I again light out toward Tarangire forest. To save time, I attempt to follow the tracks I made when coming home. It works fine as long as we are on them. But there are times we lose them in the short grass. Valuable time is lost in relocating them. This happens several times. When the light starts fading and we have lost our tracks again, I strike out to where we think the dead zebras must be. They should not be too difficult to find.

We search the sky for signs of circling vultures. They usually are not far from the kill. There are none. Where is the herd of zebras that had hung around, even after I had shot the two? Yes, aren't those the three baobab trees that were not far from where the first zebra fell? Let us take a look. Nothing. Maybe they are those three over there? Search as we do, we cannot find the zebras, dead or alive.

It is suddenly dark. Had not noticed that it was this late. So intent have I been on searching for the zebras that my eyesight has gotten accustomed to the changing light. My watch shows it is a couple of minutes past seven. Once the equatorial sun has disappeared, darkness follows swiftly on its heels! It is now going to get much darker.

I now have to find our way home. The hunt for the dead zebras has to be shelved. Now which direction is home? In our search, I have been driving in every direction, so now I am completely disoriented. I choose to set off toward a few fading red streaks in the sky, which I spot above the distant treetops.

That must be west and the station is to the southwest. Soon the red disappears altogether. After swerving around one tree and then another, I am sure that I no longer am going in the direction that had been west a few moments ago. I ask those with me which way is west; I receive a different answer from each one. They too are lost!

The headlights pick up some glowing eyes. Am told it is a lion. Those in back of the vehicle all crawl inside now. We are jammed solid. Next we see an aardvark. He is huge in the light. I have never seen one before, due to his nocturnal habits. Hit a few holes and logs, which jar everyone inside. Decrease my speed still more. Do not want to wreck something on the vehicle out here at night! My watch now shows eight-thirty. Marion will be getting concerned by now at my delay. I look at the petrol gauge, and it reads almost empty! Something has to be done and done quickly.

I stop and get out of the vehicle. Look at the sky. If I were back in western Canada, I would pick out the North Star and then know the direction to take to get out of here. But this is Tanganyika, south of the equator. The North Star is not visible in the southern hemisphere. Thus far I have not familiarized myself with the stars on this side of the world. I am lost. Test the direction of the breeze by tossing up some dust. It should be originating from the east at this time of the year, but here in the middle of the forest the dust drifts first this way and then in that direction. Give up on this experiment.

There is one more thing left for me to do if we are going to get out tonight. That is to drive in a circle, ever widening it as we go. In this way, we will, sooner or later, come to the edge. This, of course, means going deeper into the forest. We may run into a herd of elephants, or we may run out of petrol!

A few minutes later, the vehicle stops. The fuel gauge registers empty! Luckily, there is a spare gallon behind the front seat. Only one! That I drain into the tank. Well, that gives us about an hour more. I'd better get out before then.

Now and then, we come across eyes shining in the headlights. It is very dark. The moon has not risen yet. Suddenly, everything drops away in front of us! I stop at the edge of a dry riverbed. This must be the Tarangire River. So if I follow it downstream, I will reach the Great North Road. Many wild fig trees skirt the banks, which make it difficult to stay close to it. The surroundings I find myself in are unfamiliar. It either looks different at night or else I have never come up this far.

Often I stray off course, due to the heavy undergrowth and palmettos blocking my way. Even so, I keep in a westerly direction. When it appears I am straying too much, I switch to my left until the riverbed or the wild fig trees can be seen in the headlights. I am tempted to strike off in a straight line and not follow the riverbed for fear of running into elephants or buffalo. Yet I restrain myself from doing it. I cannot give up what I have. Too easy to get disoriented again. How deep are we yet in the forest?

Then through the trees we see a single light out in the distance! What is it doing out there? We get out of the vehicle and watch. Yes, it is the light of a vehicle traveling on the Great North Road! We jump back into the vehicle, and I aim it in that direction. In spite of trees blocking my way and the light finally disappearing from sight, I know we shall make it now. Soon the forest starts to thin out, and eventually we are out in the open. Thank God we have made it before running out of petrol! It is now nine-thirty. There must be only a few drops left in the tank!

Pulling into the station, I find the geologist from the potash mine five miles up the road in our yard. He is just leaving to commence searching for me! He and his wife had come earlier for a visit, and when I did not show up, he had gone back to his camp for men and a spotlight. He then returned to check whether I had come back in the meantime, before starting off into the forest. That must have been his vehicle's light we had seen when we were back in the forest! Indirectly, he had helped us find our way home.

Chapter Fifteen

Poaching?

I am sure that for most hunters there has been a safari that has left a sour note in his memory, one that he wishes he could forget somehow or erase. It is an experience we do not repeat too often, if ever, around the camp fire or in our living room when friends ask for something on Africa. Is this the reason why this chapter appears so near the end of my book?

Tarangire Game Reserve (now a national park) is a few miles beyond the Great North Road, east of our station. There is excellent hunting in the strip between the road and the reserve which includes Lake Burungi. Much of our game meat comes from this locality. When out there, you must keep your eyes open for the markers which are spaced along the boundary of the reserve. The markers are disks nailed onto a baobab or some other large tree. Even though they are painted white, you have to be observant to notice them. Not only do you have to keep your eyes on the game, but also on the posted signs, while hunting.

I am accompanying one of my colleagues out to this hunting area today. He needs to take meat back with him to his station and has asked me to go with him. The children are along as well. It is not often we get an opportunity to be on a hunt together with our children. Since this is for wildebeests or any other antelope we come across, we take them with us.

120

They are excited and are looking forward to viewing the game on this safari.

After we pass the three pyramidal hills, we enter the wooded area north of Lake Burungi. Immediately a herd of wildebeests is sighted and I stop the vehicle. My colleague commences to stalk the herd. They are nervous and show him their heels, disappearing into the shelter of the trees. The children and I wait awhile before pulling up to where we can see what is happening. Do not want to get too close to the herd with the vehicle, as this spooks them more than someone on foot. We see dust up ahead. They must still be running.

The wildebeests often walk and run in single file. I have also seen them trot around with heads held high while I was hunting them on the flats near Lake Manyara. There they associate with the zebras and Thomson gazelles. Wildebeests are mostly seen in large herds, whether on the grassy plains near the lake or in open woodland. This animal is of a clumsy appearance, often described as having the forequarters of an ox, the hindquarters of an antelope, the tail of a horse, and the horns of Cape buffalo. The Wambugwe tell us that Satan put together this beast from the leftover pieces after God had finished creating the animals!

While watching some of the Grant gazelles, we hear a shot. It comes from farther in the bush. We drive in that direction and soon find my friend with a wildebeest lying at his feet. He has brought a couple of men along with him, and they now help us load the dead animal into the pickup. My friend has a license for another wildebeest, and to make his trip worthwhile, he strides after the running herd for his second animal.

Once again, we sit and wait. The forenoon wears on. The children interest themselves with spotting various birds. The hornbills are plentiful; their continuous "wot, wot, wot, wot,

wot" fills the air. This is to me the call of the Tanganyika bush. A shot echoes through the trees! It comes from quite a distance. Bumping along toward where we had heard it, we run into the herd stampeding our way. They swing by us, dust filling the air. Then, from out of nowhere, appear two Landrovers.

They come careening over the rough terrain and stop in the opening beside me. The vehicles contain Europeans. One jumps out of the lead Landrover and walks swiftly over to me. Opening my door, he orders me to step out. Says he is the game warden and that I am poaching in the reserve. While the children look on wild-eyed, he searches the vehicle for a weapon. Finding none, he asks where I have it hidden. I repeat my earlier statement, that I do not have one with me. "There is a friend of mine out there somewhere hunting; it is his animal that you see here in the vehicle," I tell him. It all seems to be a made-up story to the warden. He believes I am the one who has killed the wildebeest. Neither does he accept the word of the two men with me. He orders them to remove the animal from the pickup.

Meanwhile, two heavyset men from the second Landrover have erected a tripod and are busily taking movies of the "poacher" and his catch. The game warden is accommodating and keeps up a running commentary of how I was caught poaching in a game reserve. No attention is paid to my explanations that I did not shoot the animal and that, as far as I know, I have not entered the reserve. When I attempt to pull the vehicle over into the shade, as the children are getting extremely hot parked under the scorching sun, the warden rushes to my door, believing I am making a run for it!

On a fourth European, who is without his shirt, there is a long scar which slants across his back. He appears to be the client, as he is giving orders to the two men with the movie equipment. They all freely drink beer from cans, tossing them aside when empty. They are enjoying themselves immensely on my behalf.

In the distance we then hear a rifle shot. The game warden cocks his head. Will he now believe me? He rushes to his vehicle and speeds in the direction the shot came from, all in less than a minute. We watch him disappear among the trees. He went alone, leaving the other three to keep their eye on me and the children, lest we should try to leave the scene.

The man with the scar on his back steps forward and addresses me, saying, "Do you know who I am?" I answer that I do not. He then gives me a name which convinces me the man is drunk! Surely he cannot be the one he claims to be. I cannot picture a prince with such behavior.

"I am the prime minister of Canada," I reply. May as well humor him.

He recoils angrily. "I am going to report you to your prime minister next time I visit him."

"Do you want his address?" I ask.

By now he is thoroughly upset with me. "What is your name and where do you live?" he demands.

I tell him. Just then, we hear a vehicle approaching, which brings an end to this ridiculous dialogue.

The Landrover screeches to a halt in front of us. Through the haze and dust I recognize the game warden and my colleague inside. The warden leaps out and relates how he found this man miles inside the game reserve with a dead wildebeest at his feet. He then had promptly confiscated his weapon and fetched him back here, leaving the shot animal lying where it fell for the vultures and jackals to devour.

The warden now attempts to drag a confession from us stating that we were hunting within the reserve. We steadfastly deny the charge. He points out the white marker on a tree about two hundred yards away, saying, "That proves you are inside the reserve!"

We then plead, "If we are, we then crossed unknowingly and had no intention of hunting in the reserve."

Enraged, the man with the scar approaches us and, picking up a dry branch, shrieks, "You ought to be whipped!"

My friend turns his back to him and says, "Go ahead."

This defuses the man and he lets go of the stick. The warden interrupts, "You may now go and in time you will hear from the law. A subpoena will be delivered to you by an officer as to the date you two are to appear in court."

With that ringing in our ears we leave this distasteful scene behind. The children are even more thankful than we are that it finally is all over. Their exciting trip has ended on a sour note.

On the way, my colleague asks me whether I know who the client was with the game warden. I answer him that I do not know. He goes on to say that the man with the scar on his back was a member of royalty (whose name I will not mention here nor the country where he resides) and the two big men with him were his personal guards! And all along I thought he was a drunkard and a braggart. No wonder he was upset when I asked him whether he needed my prime minister's address. He had been there! All of a sudden I feel sick inside.

We go to see the district commissioner up in Mbulu, a fine British gentleman, and brief him on our dilemma. We want to know whether we stand a chance with the Game Department, especially since royalty is involved. How can we get them to see that we did not enter the reserve intentionally? He advises us to backtrack our safari of that day and find out if we had entered or not. He volunteers to go with us.

It is not difficult to locate our tracks, and soon we arrive at the spot I was detained by the game warden. To our relief, we discover that we now are standing near the boundary, but outside the reserve! I see the white disk the game warden had pointed out that day to demonstrate to me that I was inside.

It suddenly dawns on me the only way you can read the marker, or even see it, is to be on the outside! If you are within the reserve the sign is on the opposite side of the tree! I was outside the reserve the whole time they were photographing me.

My colleague then retraces his steps using the tracks of the warden's vehicle. It runs parallel to the reserve boundary. The site where the second wildebeest fell is outside as well. It is comforting to have it verified that we were not poaching, as the warden had led us to believe. Will the judge believe us? The district commissioner says he will assist us as much as possible.

As the day for us to appear in court draws nearer, our friends whenever we meet offer encouragement by promising to visit us while we're behind bars. An article appears in the Arusha newspaper with the heading: "Missionaries Poaching?"

"What's going to happen, Daddy?" my daughter asks.

"God is going to make it right," I answer her.

The day of the trial arrives, and we gather in the Arusha courtroom. I feel tense and yet grateful that this day has finally arrived. The two of us are asked to stand in the box. The charge is read: "Entering the game reserve in a vehicle without permission, carrying a firearm within the game reserve, and killing an animal within the game reserve." My offense: being an accomplice to the offender.

The judge addresses me first. Asks me whether I had entered the Tarangire Game Reserve on that specific day. I reply that I had not. He then turns to my colleague and asks him the identical question. The answer is the same. The judge now asks the prosecution to bring forth the first witness. He is the game warden. But he is not present. The next witness is called for, who happens to be the prince. He has not shown up either. They both are on safari. The judge is infuriated.

"What is this anyway?" he roars at the prosecutor. After a short deliberation, he throws the case out of court. We are acquitted!

We are two jubilant men as we leave the courthouse. The outcome is an answer to prayer. We drive up Main Street praising our Lord! Oh, yes, there is a follow-up article in the newspaper stating that we have been acquitted.

A Waterbuck

The Puku I Got on the Kilombero

A Charging Rhino

A Zebra

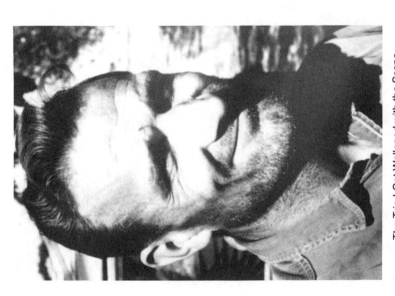

The Trip I Got Walloped with the Scope

Ostrich for New Year's Day Dinner

A Mountain Reedbuck

A Wild Hunting Dog

A Grant Gazzelle

A Warthog

A Bushpig

An Oryx

The Elusive Gerenuk

The Magnificent Greater Kudu

Homeward Bound with the Meat

Elephants in the Tarangire River near Lake Burungi

The Three Pyramidal Hills in Mbugwe

The View from Top of Them

The Hoffman Family

Chapter Sixteen

A Night to Remember

It is evening and we have a seventy-five-mile trip planned to
Arusha come morning. The two missionary families we have
had as guests for the past few days will then be leaving us as
well. The big question we are concerned with right now is
whether the men will be able to run out to a water hole near
Sangaiwe Ridge, then come back for the ladies and still get
them to town for some of their shopping by noon.

Of course, we talk ourselves into it. We will go the fifteen
miles to the water hole and check it out. If the story is correct
that a good elephant herd comes there to drink, we will follow
them up, drop one, dig out his tusks, and be back by nine. We
will have to get up early, though, and be there at dawn (which
is six here in Mbugwe). Before retiring for the night, we get
our rifles, ammunition, and binoculars ready. Do not need
water or food. We will be back by midmorning at the latest,
especially if we do not find any fresh tracks. The last words we
hear from the ladies are; "Don't forget our trip to Arusha!"

We turn off the Great North Road at Mbuyu Jermani and
drive east to the southern tip of Lake Burungi (which is dry
most of the time). There is an old baobab tree at Mbuyu Jermani which the locals use as a shelter when waiting for a lift.
It has a large opening at the base where one can easily enter
its roomy interior. During the colonial days it was a famous

137

meeting place for the Germans. Hence the name Mbuyu Jermani (German baobab). From here a road forks off west that takes you to the great Rift Wall and then on up the sheer escarpment to Mbulu. This road takes one around switchbacks which can literally rip out the suspension of even a four-wheel drive vehicle!

We reach the water hole, just as planned. There are no fresh tracks. So that's that! This means an early start to Arusha. That ought to make the women happy. Before bidding farewell to this lonely spot, we pull out our binocs and glass Sangaiwe Ridge. I have never been up there. Never had any cause to climb it. Instantly we see two large bull elephants posing for us near the crest of the ridge. Their ivory gleams in the early morning sun. They beckon us to come and get them! We talk it over some. "You know we can get up there, pop one, and then still be back in time to take the ladies to town for shopping at two o'clock. The shops are closed at noon anyway," I say.

Things do not go too well almost from the start. We struggle through bramble bush, thorns clawing us at every move. The hillside is covered with the stuff! Halfway up, I mention, "It is ridiculous to go any farther; we are not making any time at all. At this rate it will be noon before we get up there. Then, by the time we remove the tusks after we shoot him, it will be two o'clock. Besides that, we then will have to come back through all this again! By then it will be much too late to go to town."

We do not turn back. The reasoning is that we have come this far already. The Arusha trip will just have to be an evening one now—sleep there and shop tomorrow.

We push on and arrive after an uncomfortable forenoon of scrambling up the thorny hillside. We were by no means quiet forcing our way through the dry brush and wait-a-bit thorns. Anything nearby surely has heard us. There are no

138

two bulls where they had been sighted previously. They must have moved. Nothing else to do but find them. We did not come all this way for nothing!

There are more trees up here than we had seen from the base of the ridge. We realize this when we come around a bend and walk right into a herd. They had been hidden from us until this moment. Several elephants are right in front of us! They are not frightened at all, but keep going about their feeding. Must not have been hunted in the past. Surveying them, as some browse off the trees and others lumber nonchalantly across the opening, we see no tusks worth the bother. The herd is mainly cows and calves. The two bulls we had spotted earlier are not around. They may be on the outskirts of the herd. So we work our way around them. Nothing. Maybe they are farther along. We move on up the trail that winds along the crest of the ridge. The sun is now directly above us. We are hot and thirsty!

The next opening we come to has two rhino in it, a cow and her half-grown calf. She is alert instantly and turns to face us. Where the elephants are docile, the rhino is not. She charges us and we scatter. I make it to the top of a large boulder before she catches me. The young one looks on in bewilderment. After a few more snorts, the mother turns and trots off, her tail pointing straight up, much like a flagpole. The calf tags after her into the trees. Now we have to keep an eye open for rhino as well!

At two in the afternoon, we begin talking about returning to the vehicle, which is now miles back at the foot of the ridge. We are parched! Why didn't we at least bring a canteen of water? Of course, originally, we had not planned to come up here. Upon hearing us talk about turning back, our guide, whom we had picked up at the village below, now tells us there is a spring up here on Sangaiwe Ridge, a good-sized one with plenty of fresh water and just ahead of us on the trail. That is the best news all day! It sounds so good that already I can taste the cool water. We agree to go to it, fill up, return to the vehicle, and be back home by dark.

We march and march and march! No spring. By four we are getting irritated with the guide, who keeps insisting that it is just ahead. At six, we do not believe him anymore. There probably isn't even a spring up here at all! Too far along the way to turn back, so we march on. We are weak with dehydration. Fifteen minutes later we see it! Actually, it is the elephants we see first. There are many of them gathered at the water, which is seeping out from the base of a huge projecting boulder.

The elephants do not interest us at all right now, but the water does. If they notice us, they do not reveal it. There is no trumpeting, no stampede, just a carefree herd enjoying the evening. A few at the spring are spraying water on themselves with their trunks, and I yearn for some of it. But we have to drive them away first so as to enjoy it, too. Before we start doing that, we must secure ourselves a location where we will be safe in case of a sudden change in the attitude of the herd. The top of the knoll, where the projecting boulder is, looks like the best spot.

Leaving the concealment of the trees, we tread cautiously into the open glade. There are even more *tembo* to our right, which we had not noticed before. They too ignore us. We reach the knoll without any interference from them and go up it unchallenged. From the top we are able to see those at the spring right below us, others scattered throughout the glade, and still more among the trees beyond. There must be at least fifty elephants about us!

To spook the *tembo* away from the water, we shoot off a round into the air. They stop, listen, and then resume their activities. How different from the usual! Ordinarily, none would be left now. They would all be fleeing madly through the trees. Yet there they are. Not one has the urge to leave. We fire several more rounds. Still no reaction. Finally, we send a few bullets thudding into the mud at their feet. They back off at this and move away from the water. Not too disturbed, they join the ones who are quitting the glade to seek forage in the trees.

We descend the knoll and dash to the spring. On all fours, we guzzle the water until our thirst subsides, then we soak our heads. We feel renewed! It will be dark in less than an hour; we must therefore hurry to get the bull with the long tusks. While on top, we had spotted one worthwhile bull standing back in the trees. Even his ivory is not that heavy, but he is the best in the whole herd.

It is dusk when we complete extracting the tusks. It had not taken us long to catch up to the bull and drop him. On our way back to the spring, we are wondering where we will spend the night. Scanning the trees along the way, we see none that we could climb into for the night. Very few have any sturdy forks, and those that do are too near the ground. The only other place of reasonable safety in this beautiful but forsaken land is the knoll. We mount it in the dark and stretch out on the ledge overlooking the spring.

Everything is black around us. We try to nestle in and get some sleep, but the ground does not lend itself to that. Besides the guide, we have a Bushman with us. He is now lying near me curled up, his head resting on one of the tusks, fast asleep. Nothing will wake him now until morning. He will sleep the sleep of the dead, as they call it. He is the only one in our group that has had anything to eat. While cutting out the tusks, he had helped himself to bits of meat, eating it raw. He also scraped off the gristle from the tusks and ate it while waiting for sleep.

There is a breeze and it is getting cold up here on the ridge. I am only wearing a short-sleeved shirt. I am reminded of the time we spent a night out on a ridge in Yaida Valley. We had also gotten caught far from our vehicle and so had to spend the night among some rocks. I was very cold that night, in spite of huddling in a crevice. Morning did not come any too soon for me. Had hyenas prowling around throughout the night.

The elephants have returned and are at the spring. We cannot see them, only hear them and at times almost feel them. They know we are here, for often a trunk appears and almost reaches us where we sit. We are that close to them! At ten, there is a shuffling to my left! An elephant is approaching our roost, probably sent to investigate. We have our rifles ready. He stops a short distance away. Too dark to see anything. After minutes of silence, I start to relax and breathe normally. We hear no further footsteps, coming or going. Tembo simply melted away like a phantom.

There is loud splashing at the spring around midnight. Bellowing and snorting, a herd of buffalo mill about for some time. It must be a large herd by the sounds of it. Let's hope they do not venture up here. When the buffalo have left, the rasping cough of a leopard breaks the stillness of the night. Nearer and nearer he advances. He stops when he picks up our scent. I am sure he is crouching close by observing us right now. He is at home here; we are not. When he leaves I do not know. He is the type of animal that when you think he has gone, he is still around. When you think he is still around, he has long gone. The quietude is broken by a lion grunting, fading away into the distance. It comes from the valley below, in the direction of where we left the vehicle.

The night finally ends. I am cramped from the cold air and from not having slept. Looking over the edge, we see a rhino at the water. He is in no hurry to leave, but we are. Without any further delay, we descend to the bottom. When we are midway to the line of trees, he charges. I get behind a tree as he puffs by me in search of the others. Everyone is running for a tree! The Bushman is up one of them before any of us. The rhino is persistent and it is some time before we eventually shake him. We had to do a lot of dodging and twisting to get far enough away from him. The last we see of him, he is still testing the air.

It is noon when we arrive at the vehicle. We did not retrace our steps along the crest of the ridge, but made a gradual descent to the valley floor as soon as we had gotten rid of the rhino. Along this route we sight elephant at different points, but they fail to interest us. We want to get home as soon as possible to let the women know we are still alive. They probably wondered all day yesterday what had happened, and today they must be climbing walls!

We find the Mbugwe tribesman we had left with the vehicle still present! He has waited faithfully for our return. He said he found some groundnuts in the Landrover and ate them. Told us how lions had prowled around during the night. Must have been the ones we had heard. He too had a night to remember!

When we drop the guide at his home near Lake Burungi, his wife informs us that a European lady had come looking for us this very morning. Her car was full of kids. That must be Marion, but why did she bring the children? The lady went on to say that she (Marion) went on into the bush when she learned we had not yet returned. Oh, no! Not with a car in that bush, where elephant and rhino are wandering about! What if she has a flat?

We turn around and head back into the bush. Her tracks lead us to the water hole of yesterday morning. She has done well in reading our tracks thus far. But then she leaves our tracks and strikes off in another direction. We follow until we lose her tracks in the dry grass and underbrush. This is ridiculous! We are looking for each other, and in the process we lose each other. Why not turn back and wait for her at the guide's hut? Sooner or later she will have to show up again. As long as nothing happens in between time!

An hour later, we see dust rising above the tops of the trees back in the bush. The car appears, and soon she pulls up to where we are standing. Out jump not the children, but some of our help from the station. When the woman had said small people, I had taken for granted she meant children. I should have asked her what color they were.

Yes, Marion had seen plenty of elephants during her cruise in the bush; in fact, she had to stop for them, as they were blocking her way. Besides the *tembo*, she also met up with a rhino. Yes, she thought it was ridiculous to continue her search for us, so she came back before she got trampled or completely lost.

Finally, after thirty hours, we are reunited. Oh, yes to make amends we are still going on to Arusha today for an evening out with the ladies.

Chapter Seventeen

Empty-handed

The Kilombero River is a tributary of the mighty Rufiji in Southeast Tanganyika. Two others and I are driving down to this area for elephant. We had received a lead that some really big ones were holed up in the swampland. The huge Selous Game Reserve lies not far away; here exceptionally large tuskers roam. So we cannot go wrong by going to this secluded location.

We arrive in this isolated expanse, and I discover the surrounding scene is quite different from what I am accustomed to when elephant hunting. The landscape is flat as far as the eye can see. No hills to climb when glassing for animals. There is only tall grass, just high enough so you cannot see over it. So how are we to sight them? You have to walk up to them, we are told. When you do close in on them, we are to be careful, as the elephants here are very aggressive, they add. Well, we have come this far, we might as well give it a try. Not what I am used to, but there is always room to learn.

Since we are outsiders, we inquire about some trackers who know the area well. Of course, they all know, and we narrow the bunch down to three fellows. They are local chaps and appear to be a good-natured lot. They know where the elephants are residing and will lead us to them. Soon I am going to observe my first swamp elephants! Off we trek,

145

strung out behind the self-appointed leader of our newfound friends.

We march along for miles in the tall grass. The *tembo* are in here, somewhere, we are told. Coming upon their spoor, we notice it is not very fresh. We carry on. The next set of tracks we encounter we decide to follow. It is of a passing herd, and we never do catch up to them. We give up on them after trailing them to the river. The river is very deep, we are told. Elephants walk along the bottom, their trunks stretched overhead so they can take in air. The little ones float along behind, using their own trunks to hang onto mama's tail.

The following day is the same story, the day after as well. We just do not see any, nor do we get near enough to hear them except once. They are there, somewhere in the tall grass ahead of us. The spoor is fresh. But how do you determine where the big ones are, if there are any at all? We would need a ladder, but no one volunteers to assemble one for us. They say it is not practical. We stay on the trail for most of the day. It is hot and humid in the tall grass, but we persevere until finally they leave the swampland and venture into some trees which appear out of nowhere.

The herd travels on, crossing a small river then on into cultivated *shambas.* Here we note there are one or two footprints that look large enough to belong to beasts carrying heavy ivory. We stay on their trail, crossing numerous streams. At one the guide gets tired of standing around while we unlace and lace our boots, so he tells me to get on his back and packs me across. He is much lighter than I am but carries me without a problem. The muscles in his legs are like steel. Our procession takes us past a village where a *pombe* party is in full swing. Before we know what is happening, our guide has detached himself and is emptying a gourd of the native beer. He is back with us again before too long.

Ahead of us is a growth of trees and in it our herd. We

have finally overtaken them. After inspection, we conclude that there is not one *tembo* worth shooting. A few of them are big, but their tusks are small. We have used up the better part of a day trailing a worthless herd! There is a village nearby, and we head for it. We need new information. Were there any elephants raiding their *shambas*?

At dusk, we reach the village, which is tucked away in the remoteness of this vast swampland. The inhabitants welcome us warmly, and we are offered three-legged stools to sit on while a woman brings us water to drink. She kneels before us and respectfully offers the gourd with both hands. The women in this tribe, I notice, kneel when meeting the opposite sex. Earlier, as we were approaching the village, those we met on the path stepped off and knelt until we had passed. I was told this was the custom here. I wonder how my wife would adjust to a custom such as this. It certainly does something to the male ego!

The huts in the village are built on stilts. This is to keep the vermin and the snakes out of the grain bins and sleeping quarters. It, of course, does not help against the larger animals such as the marauding elephants which come at night.

"Do they come often?" we ask.

"Yes, they came last night and are expected to return tonight, as this is the season when they remain in the area for weeks."

We resolve to keep an eye open tonight.

We bed down on the ground in the center of the village compound. We have adjusted to sleeping on the hard earth. It has been several days since we left our vehicle back in a fisherman's village at the fringe of the swamp. I again scoop out a hollow for my hip or buttocks, depending how I lie when I sleep. It makes it more restful. My pillow is the water canteen wrapped in my slicker.

It is midnight when we hear the elephants. They are on

the outskirts of the village. We cannot distinguish whether there are any real tuskers in the herd, as the moon will not rise for another two hours. I crouch down on all fours to get a glimpse of their shapes against the sky (which is a bit paler than the dark landscape). But it is not light enough to distinguish their tusks. We listen to them forage on the vegetation and decide to follow them at daybreak.

The elephants do not enter the compound. They may have sensed something out of the ordinary. We easily pick up the spoor at dawn and set out after them. It leads into the swamp, which does not suit us at all. But we are determined to give it our best for a couple of hours. Beating our way through the tall bulrushes, we again come to the Kilombero River. Their tracks reveal they have forded it. Let us get on this river as soon as we come across someone with a canoe is our next plan. We do not go far before we meet some fishermen who have a canoe. It is a long dugout, and we all fit into it nicely.

They paddle us in and out of small inlets along the Kilombero, but we see no sign of elephants. Hippos are plentiful, though, and we are in view of them almost constantly. They stare at us in the swift moving canoe. We could easily have hippo meat tonight if we had the time. But to wait until they come up after shot, then drag them to shore and cut out a steak will delay us too much. We do take time to go after a puku, a medium-sized antelope, which are numerous on the open glades beside the river. None of us brought along a small caliber rifle, so it fell to me to shoot it with my .458 (as I have a scope along).

The puku are skittish and will not allow me to approach them. I take a long shot and get whacked on my forehead with the scope! I failed to keep in mind the kick of the big gun. Blood flows from a neat cut above my eye. There is some consolation in that I dropped the animal. There is now meat for the pot this evening. We dump the carcass in the canoe and carry it to the fishermen's camp. Here it is skinned and dressed.

While this is being done, I strip and wade into the river for a bath. About time I have one! When the fishermen spot me in the water, they frantically beckon me to return to the bank. They shout to me there are crocodiles in the river! Especially right here, as this is where they dump the remains of the fish. Needless to say, I heed their warning and finish my wash nearer shore with an attentive eye on the flowing Kilombero, wherein countless crocodiles do lurk.

The next day, we cruise farther along the river. It is peaceful and relaxing, but no *tembo*. In the evening, we have the canoe men drop us off at a high point beside the Kilombero. The vehicle is across the swampland, about a day's march from here. We will start tomorrow and head in that direction. If we do not come across any elephants or notice any fresh spoor, we will call an end to our safari and leave for home. Our bed is again the hard ground. The only shelter around us is a sparsely thatched shed, which the fishermen use to smoke and dry their fish, hardly a refuge from the pending rain. There has been rumbling and some flashes of lightning in the distance. Clouds are also moving in from the east.

Fortunately, it does not rain and we awaken to a clear sky. It will be another hot day. This is our last day here in the Kilombero swamp, unless of course we meet up with a good tusker. We peer into the bulrushes, we strain our ears, yet no sign of elephants! We reach our vehicle by nightfall. The villagers come to see the tusks we do not have. Despite striking out, we are in good spirits. We bed down beside the vehicle for the night amid many onlookers.

I arrive home unkempt and unshaven. All I have to show for my safari to the Kilombero is a week-long growth of beard and a welt on my forehead from the scope. Marion refuses to kiss me at the door until I have had a shave and a hot bath. Is it that bad?

I need to say here that not every hunt ends successfully. It is just that we like to relate the ones which do. There are many safaris that are fruitless and cause you to return empty-handed.

Chapter Eighteen

At Last!

An animal I have stalked for miles on foot is the greater kudu. I wanted a male carrying sizable horns, but he kept endlessly eluding me. The more I tried and failed, the more determined I became to get one, no matter how long it would take.

There are numerous greater kudu in Uburunge, where we have a station. Often I have seen them leap across the road when I was returning in the evening. Yet a good-sized male was never in the midst of them. Once I did stop and follow up three of them, as we needed meat. When they stopped to look back, I dropped the best one of the bunch. The horns, though, were not what I wanted to adorn my wall.

The favorite haunts of the greater kudu are in thick bush or light forests. They are seen in hilly country, avoiding the open plains. Resting in the shade of trees during the heat of the day, they feed from late afternoon to early morning, often invading fields of farmers nearby. The kudu are very sensitive to sound and when alarmed can jump barriers much higher than themselves. Their call is a loud, hoarse bark. A large antelope, the male stands over five feet at the shoulders and weighs up to seven hundred pounds. There are white stripes on each side of his grayish body, and his long horns spread outward in open spirals—a truly magnificent-looking beast!

Time went on; every now and then I would sight them or would be informed of their nearby whereabouts and pursue the large-racked male. Mostly I would return tired and empty-handed. Once I encountered one with a beautiful set of horns while I was hunting elephants. He stood long enough for me to have a good look. Then he was gone. Had I been carrying my 30-06, I may have been tempted to shoot him, but right then I was after elephants. You learn not to get side-tracked when after big game, unless there is a need for meat for the men in your safari.

Salimu, a very good tracker, arrives one morning and informs me that a big male has been feeding in his *shamba* during the night. "Shall we go after him, Bwana?" He has accompanied me before and knows I want a good head.

"You think he's a big one?" I ask.

"*Ndio* [yes], his tracks reveal he's *kubwa sana* [very big]!" he answers.

"Will his horns be big?"

"*Ndio,* Bwana!"

I take my 30-06 and we stroll out to his *shamba* to inspect the tracks. Soon we are heading out into the dry countryside, Salimu in front reading the spoor, with me following close behind. At times, I see no sign at all, but Salimu knows exactly which direction the kudu is heading. On the way, the bull is joined by two females. The spoor leads us through several patches of shrubs and bushes and is getting fresher.

Then we hear what we have been straining to hear for some time, twigs snapping! It comes from a stand of dry trees ahead of us. Drawing nearer to it, we hear them exit on the far side. We sprint around the bush only to find them disappearing into the next stand of trees. Gingerly we make our way to the spot they have entered. Discovering thick underbrush when we get there, we cannot see more than a yard or two in front of us. In our attempt to enter the entanglement,

152

we hear them take flight once again. Dry branches crack as they barge through the underbrush. By the time we manage to withdraw ourselves, they are nowhere in sight.

Their tracks lead us to another clump of bushes. This time we circle it, planning to catch them in the act of leaving. But they already have gone. They did not tarry in this one. We keep following the kudu throughout the hot day. They go in and out of the bushes, always staying ahead of us. Occasionally we spot them just as they enter the brush, but there is not sufficient time for a shot. The duel is on!

The kudu lead us around in a large circle. We now have covered many miles and are parched. Yielding to the pangs of thirst at one stagnant pool, we drink the reddish liquid. It does not seem like the best thing to do, but I am dehydrated. Revived, we resume the pace. We are now back in the area where we first had seen the tracks of the females joining the male's.

It is past four in the afternoon. They are either tiring or getting accustomed to us tailing them, for their wariness lessens. First one female stands still until we come into view, then flees to join the others in the bush. Then the second female tarries. Finally, the male lingers a bit too long and he falls to my shot.

The horns are nice, but I have seen much better ones. Had I gotten a good view of them at the beginning of the race, I may not have taken up the chase. But I do feel triumphant, trooping along in file with those who carry the meat and horns to the station. I have ended up just three miles from where I started. Word had been sent to the workers and others along the way to come help transport the animal home.

*　　*　　*

It is months later when I am informed of a very big kudu

153

male showing up each night to browse in the *shambas* of a certain neighborhood. He has been seen on several occasions by the owners who appear at daybreak. Going to the vicinity, I inquire where he has last been sighted. They point me to a new *shamba* that has been hacked out of the bush recently. Standing in it, I notice it is enclosed with trees—an ideal feeding place for the kudu! I learn from the villagers that he returns to feed several nights in a row at one field, then moves on to the next place. He has been present the two previous nights, so I am told he will be back.

Returning before sunset, I hide myself near a spot where I think the kudu will likely feed. Sitting and watching with me is one of the villagers. Although we wait until past dusk, the kudu does not put in an appearance. With nothing further to do, I go on home, leaving word that I will come again in the morning.

When I arrive at the *shamba* just as dawn is breaking, the kudu spots me before I notice him in the misty light. He dives into the thicket and is gone. I did catch a glimpse of his horns, and they are worth coming back for, no matter how often. They are beautiful! He has been spooked, so no need to hang around. I have work waiting for me at home. I know from our previous meetings that I would not see the kudu again today. Not this one! Before leaving, I give instructions to call me whenever he reappears.

The following day, I am summoned to a *shamba* a short distance from where I had last seen the greater kudu. Arriving an hour before sunset, I wait for him as I had done previously. Again, he does not show up before dark. So I return the next morning at daybreak. Walking silently up to the edge of the trees that border the field, I spy him at the far end. It is a foggy morning, and the light is not sufficient for a clear shot. As I am debating whether I should try anyway he vanishes. I know now if I should ever see him again, I would have to make a quick shot.

We try stalking him in the heavy underbrush, but it is quite useless. We hear him often yet never quite see him. Giving up finally, we return home. Do not search for him that evening, but revisit the site the following morning. This time he is nowhere to be seen. He has moved.

Standing there, I look over the situation. Where will he feed next? There are *shambas* scattered about in the area. I have not noticed that he is following a pattern of any kind, so that does not help. There is one field that lies at the far end of the line of *shambas*. To me this could be a likely place for the bull to try on his next outing. It lies right next to a dense stand of trees. Dead brush skirts the field on two sides. This niche could give him all the advantage he needs. I decide then and there to come to this acreage in the morning.

Arising while it is still dark, I head out for my next rendezvous with the elusive kudu. Ere long I am on the path leading out to the *shamba*. The villager who has accompanied me during the last few days again joins me along the way. It is a four-mile trek. A heavy dew lies on the ground this morning. There is an air of expectancy around, and I can hardly contain myself. It dare not interfere with my aim when it comes time to shoot!

I wipe the sweat from the palm of my hands and get a fresh grip on the 30-06. My pulse is racing out of control, like a runaway horse. Now wait a minute! I should not be acting this way. It is when I am after the Big Five that I cannot shake this feeling of intense excitement. I must get ahold of myself!

Fully alert, I approach the clearing. There is not that much light yet. Surveying the scene before me, I hear a slight whisper and see the kudu leap swiftly for the edge of the field. He again spotted me before I could detect him! Upon reaching the fringe of the trees, he does something he has not done in our previous encounters. He halts and glances back. That costs him his life.

He rears high when my bullet hits him, then drops and lies still. Am I dreaming? I have run and rerun this thing over in my mind for days! Has it really happened? As I admire him lying now at my feet, he still looks regal with his huge horns reaching far back over his body. At last, I have my trophy!

Chapter Nineteen

The Herd Bull

At sunset, we pull up underneath a huge baobab tree. This is where we will set up for the night. It does not take long before our tracker is busily skinning the impala which was dropped nearby for our evening meal. No sooner have we fixed our camp and lit our fire when out of the darkness appear three Mangati women. They have come from a *manyatta* (enclosed compound) less than a mile away. The Mangati are cattle herders, much like the Masai, wandering far from their native grounds on the outskirts of Mount Hanang in search of grassland.

Two of the women have babies strapped on their backs. They silently watch us prepare our evening meal, interested in everything we do. Noticing we have left behind our kettle for heating the water, one of my companions asks the curious leather-clad beauties, *"Sisi hatuna bikira hapa; tafadali tusaidie moja usiku huu."* No sooner had he ended his request when my other companion (Merv) and I explode in laughter while the women remain sober-faced. Instead of saying, "We do not have a kettle here; please help us with one tonight," he had said, "We do not have a virgin here, please help us with one tonight." *Kettle* in Swahili is *birika* and not *bikira.* It was a slip of the tongue. After we correct his mistake, the women join us this time in the second round of laughter.

Oh! Did we get a kettle? No, they did not possess one. They say that they have a *sufuria* (metal pot), though, which they could lend us. But since we have one of these along ourselves, we end up using that to brew our tea. It does not matter anymore whether the occasional *dudu* (insect) lands in our pot. Earlier I had noticed a squadron of them, after being overcome by smoke from the open fire, spiral headlong into our soup. Anyway, who is fussy out here in the Tanganyika bush?

*   *   *

I have a beautiful pair of symmetrically shaped tusks in my possession. I highly prize these trophies. When I look at them I am reminded of the day I got the elephant that carried them. He was the herd bull.

We have been watching the elephants all day. There are at least a hundred of them in the herd. The cows and their calves of all sizes are scattered everywhere in the valley beneath us. We are up among the rocks overlooking them. Other bulls are there as well, but tend to stay away from the immediate presence of the herd bull. This big bull stands above all the rest. He is not yet old enough to start living a solitary life.

Yet, he is still capable of handling a herd. Whenever he screams a command there is obedience. It is quite interesting, fascinating as well, to watch their movements throughout the day. They do not stray much. There is plenty to eat, and so they browse. Younger ones are lively and mischievous. Just then I see the big one jab another bull in the rump. He does not accept him being in the inner circle. I want this herd bull! He is carrying two beautifully shaped tusks.

During the noonday heat, they settle down under large, shady acacia trees, where they now stand with heads bowed and ears slowly swinging to and fro. We search for an opening to creep up to the monarch. There are some holes in the stand of trees ahead of us. We steal down the rocks to the base and discover we cannot see the elephants too well, due to the tall underbrush. Some of us climb the trees to get a better view. It still is not as good as where we had been, so we return to our perch on the rocks.

We are able to ascend and descend these rocks without any undue hardship, not like the one I will never forget from an earlier safari. I had needed to get up higher in order to glass the broken terrain for the herd that had vanished into the vast wilderness. It is because of the tracker that I find myself now among the huge boulders that rise singly above the treetops. He is a Bushman, and when a honeybird called to him, he forsook the elephants' spoor, much to my chagrin, and lit out to satisfy his sweet tooth. I could do nothing but follow him.

Despite the angry bees all about him, he continues to dig out the honey from the hole in the baobab tree. Sitting here waiting, I get a notion to climb the twenty-foot-high boulder nearby. I may just sight the *tembo* we have been tracking from up there. After reaching it, I discover it is impossible to scale due to its shape being spherical—absent of any cracks to assist me in climbing. Because of the high vegetation around it, this was not visible from a distance. There is a tree growing next to it, though, which should aid me to where I wish to go.

The branch I find myself on does not quite reach the boulder. By hanging onto the limb and swinging, much like Tarzan would have, I leap and land on top of the rock. I search the surrounding countryside, but it is empty of *tembo*. Time to return to my honey-eating friend and steer him back onto the spoor. Now how do I get down? The branch is out of reach, and sliding out over the belly of the rock will surely mean a broken leg or two. I have really done it this time!

I realize that the only way to descend is the way I came. I must leap back onto the branch that brought me here. Should I miss or the limb break, then I will have a rough re-entry to earth. I jump and grab for the branch. It swings down with my weight, but does not snap. I make my way to the trunk, pulling myself along hand over hand. Once I am there it takes only a minute and I am safely on the ground again. Phew! I will not do that again.

While we are on the subject of rocks, I am reminded of another incident. Three of us were spending a day just taking it easy on top of a boulder-strewn hillock, keeping track of the elephants in a valley below. The reason for the lack of activity is that I am suffering from malaria. Lying there in my weakened condition, I watch one of my companions shove the upper plate of his false teeth forward to see how the Bushman, our tracker, would react to it.

The Mtindiga stares in disbelief. Finally, he dares to ask, "How do you do it?"

The answer given is: "You lie back, prop your legs against the rock, and push. Why don't you try it?"

Well, the Bushman did as he was instructed, but to no avail. His teeth would not move out at all. After several more attempts, he turns to the other member of our party and asks, "Can you do what your friend just did?"

"Sure," comes the reply. "Watch." With that he places his feet against the boulder and presses.

To his great astonishment, the Bushman beholds this man's front teeth commence to project as well. (He has a partial plate.) The tracker's eyes are now about ready to pop out of their sockets. What kind of witchcraft is this?

"What about you?" he now inquires of me. "Can you do this, too?"

I faintly answer, "No, I do not have enough strength today because of my illness."

He does not persist. But had he, I would have failed the test, as all my teeth are still well rooted. We no longer can keep a straight face, and the laughter that has been held in check now bursts forth. Yes, he eventually is given an explanation to this great phenomenon. But do you know that he fancied the former rendition? That is a fact, for when he felt no one was watching, he was on his back pushing with all his might, determined to accomplish this feat.

I have since recuperated from my bout with malaria and am back to my normal self. At the moment, I am anxious to get this herd bull below us. Thus far a real opportunity to do so has yet to present itself. We could do what we have done on a few previous occasions. That is, walk into the herd and pick out the one we want! We have done it when they browsed or rested in ravines with shrubs so high you could only see their backs. We would sneak into their midst, moving cautiously from one to another, until we had examined all the ivory. It works when there is not any breeze at all. Should one suddenly stir when you are still down among them, they will stampede. It is then you freeze near a good sized tree or a termite mound or race with them if you have spotted one you want! Of course, you only do this when you are desperate, after all other methods have failed. Right now, we are not that desperate.

At four, the tightly knit groups begin breaking up and several lumber over to one of the trees we had climbed previously. They examine it suspiciously. Getting bolder, they grasp the branches with their trunks and shake the tree. Had we remained up there, we would now have to contend with some very disturbed cows! Others move near to the rocks where we are seated. One of the bulls in that group is carrying reasonable tusks. Should we take him and forget the herd bull? I turn my gaze over to the monarch, and he is still surrounded by most of the herd. Time is running out. Before long the sun will be across the distant ridge. The vehicle is miles away, which means we have to do something real quick.

Just then, someone from our group shoots at the one below us. The angle is bad and it is a miss. There is now a stampede in the valley below us. Elephants are running everywhere, over one hundred of them! The herd bull is attempting to direct them along the foot of the ridge that we are on and then out through the opening into the forest beyond. We start running along the rise, attempting to keep pace with them, longing now for a shot at any good one.

Running full out, we notice a section of the herd turn abruptly and come up the rise in our direction! What to do now? There are too many to make a stand, too many cows and calves to cope with, and a decision has to be made swiftly. During the mad dash after the stampede started, most of us had gotten separated from each other. I now see my two companions and gun bearers scampering up into some high rocks. One of them loses his hat.

As I am standing there taking my last look at the herd fleeing with their leader and then at the bunch charging up toward us, the tracker who has stuck with me touches my arm. He points ahead to the opening at the end of the ridge to where the herd bull is aiming his elephants. "If we hurry," he says, "we will get there at the same time!" He and I shoot out across the broken terrain, disregarding the approaching group from our left. By the time they get to the top, we are gone, and they pass behind us in wake of my two fleeing companions.

I reach the edge of the ridge just as the herd comes rushing through the opening. They are on their way to the forest. I am not close enough to get off the shot I would like. I watch them as they exit parallel to us, soon to be lost in the miles and miles of thick Yaida bushland. Suddenly the big one comes into view! He is on my side of the herd. What a beauty!

If I were only a little closer to him. He is at least two hundred yards from me and running hard. There is just one shot I can make now, and I take it.

The bull staggers and misses a couple of strides, but keeps sticking with the herd. We stand watching from the top of the rise. Did I hit the heart? Yes, I have! We see him stop just inside the line of trees. His back legs give way, and he comes to rest on his rump. Several gather around him and attempt to raise him to his feet. But he is unable to stand alone without their assistance. Then the gallant beast pierces the still evening air with a scream that echoes and re-echoes throughout the whole valley below. The elephants flee as though ordered. It was his final command! The herd bull is dead.

Besides being thrilled over conquering this fine monarch, I feel a tinge of sorrow at the passing of such a noble beast. It could easily have ended differently, as elephants are noted for assisting a wounded member of the herd in making his escape. I witnessed this while on a safari with a friend of mine in Masailand.

We were stalking a herd in a large bush area overlooking the steppe. There was plenty of cover, making it possible to get up close to them. They stood scattered somewhat before us. We had worked our way into an excellent spot. The big animal with the heavy ivory was now facing us, less than fifteen yards away. The only problem was he had several cows flanking him on either side; one of these had no tusks. Looking him straight in the eye, we each put a bullet into his massive forehead. The big fellow slumped to the ground, and the tuskless cow charged in our direction.

We ran, dodging trees, skipping over fallen limbs, expecting any moment to be swept up by the enraged female. Tuskless females are the worst to encounter. Through the years they have discovered that man does not want them, for they carry no ivory. So they readily turn on him and have successfully ruined many a hunt. Almost every herd contains one of these fearless creatures.

The shrieking and the trumpeting grow fainter as we get farther away. Then the din abruptly stops. We come to a halt and listen. Should we retrace our steps? "No," says my friend, "let's give them time to disperse. We got the big one." So we wait for half an hour. When we finally return to the scene, the elephants are all gone, including the one we had shot! We see the spot where they had raised him; then he was supported by one on either side of him as they half carried, half dragged him along. They left a swath wide enough for a lorry to pass through. Trees had been knocked flat wherever they had stood in their way.

We follow their trail until dark without catching up to them. Next morning, we resumed the search. Gave up finally when the spoor vanished at the edge of an escarpment. Could find no fresh tracks leading down onto the plains. It is as if they had leaped out into space!

My two fleeing companions have now returned and join me at the side of this fallen herd bull who had failed to escape. Even in death he still looks dignified and majestic. His tusks are evenly matched. Often you find where one will be shorter or lighter than the other tusk. I determine to keep this set, to remind me of this successful hunt and particularly the noble beast who carried them.

The Watindiga have started to filter in one by one. Some sentinels have been watching us for hours, perched on high points where they can view for miles in every direction. When my elephant went down the ululating had started, from hilltop to treetop until the news had reached the villages. Soon this carcass will be cut up and then eaten on the spot. One of them is ecstatic, jigging and sucking the juice out of the bone splinters chopped from the elephant's head. There would be no merriment now, had I failed to drop the herd bull.

It is dark as we start out for the vehicle, miles away. We are a tired and a quiet lot as we hurry along, walking briskly, hoping that we are on course. A large shape appears before us. There is no moon out, so we cannot distinguish much ahead of us. Drawing nearer, we realize it is not the top of a distant baobab but an elephant! He is standing directly in our path, a few paces ahead of us. We listen and hear others. We have walked into the herd that has just lost their leader!

Let me say at this point that elephants are not timid at night but quite aggressive. We therefore have to be extremely careful now. It is obvious that we cannot go any farther without running the risk of being noticed by them. What are we to do? The Bushman who is escorting us whispers to us that we should follow him. He moves stealthily over to our left until we come to a huge baobab. *Tembo* are everywhere. He ushers us through an opening into the base of the tree. He says that he uses it when out in search of honey.

It is spacious inside, enough room for us all. This is to be our lodging place tonight. It does not take long before we find that we are not the only occupants. All night bats bombard us, their odor stifling in our windowless apartment. Oh, well, you cannot have everything. At least we are safe from the elephants, who are wandering around out there without their chief. No, I will not forget him!

Chapter Twenty

The Water Hole

The mother warthog, her tail sticking straight up like an antenna, trots quickly across our road into the dry grass. Behind her follow six young ones. Like mama, their little tails are erect as they trot along in a line, one behind the other. They are on their way to the water hole—only a stone's throw from where I sit on our front step. It is the dry season. Already there have been grass fires. As I gaze out across the savanna it looks quite bleak. There are patches of dry grass here and there that the fire has not burned. Young palm trees (palmettos) have been scorched by the flames but will survive. In spite of yearly fires, a sight to behold, especially at night, life on the savanna and in the bush carries on. Sitting here in the cool of the day as the sun quickens its pace to hide behind the Rift Wall, I can see a variety of animals making their way to the water hole to slake their thirst at the end of a very hot day.

Baboons are the noisiest, especially when someone or something disturbs them, such as a reedbuck springing up suddenly, whistling sharply, then darting off only to lie down again somewhere else in the tall grass. The sentry baboon perched on a termite mound or high up on a branch of an old fig tree barks loudly. The francolins flutter up, shrilling loudly. They are extremely noisy at dusk. The yellow-necked spurfowl is a regular visitor here each morning and evening. His loud, grating "graark, grak, grak" is part of the Tangayika bush.

The stately giraffes amble along slowly, pausing frequently to stare at something in the distance. They enjoy feeding on the nearby thorn trees, which they have no problem reaching with their long necks. The giraffe is Marion's favorite animal. He is no threat to anyone in spite of being the tallest animal in the world. One without a tail has been seen now and then. The Masai have told us they sneaked up to the giraffe when he was down resting and hacked off his tail before he could get up. The tail then became a fly whisk for an elder in the tribe. Throughout the day, at any time, we can see a number of giraffes from our front veranda. At night they move across the compound. Our phone wire running between the buildings had to be heightened, as it was torn down one night by a wandering giraffe.

There are zebras nearby. Just heard one of them bark. When the rains begin, they will not be as numerous here, as they fancy being with the wildebeests, who only show up this far occasionally. They prefer the open flats near the lake two miles away. The first animal we saw when we chose this site for our station was the zebra. They were feeding under the huge fig tree standing here with the elephant tusk marks on it.

Near the compound is a jungle of greenery wherein the waterbuck take refuge. Soon I will see their long, crescent curved horns show above the tall grass as they move silently toward the water hole. They are never far from water. The bushbuck is hiding along the riverbed in the dense brush. He is very shy and elusive, not moving more than a short distance from where he has spent the day. He will go to the water hole tonight for his drink. His voice is a loud, clear bark which sounds so much like that of the baboon. Bushbuck are a favorite prey of the leopard, who will be passing through here at dusk. Right now he is hiding among the rocks on one of the

167

pyramidal hills. It will not be long now before I will hear his rasping cough, which sounds like someone sawing wood. Even though he primarily hunts at night, I did see one in broad daylight climb up a fig tree just off our compound, dragging a dead reedbuck, and hang him across a fork in the branch. He then commenced feeding on him. This is his territory.

Though very numerous, dik-diks are difficult to observe. Being mostly nocturnal, they soon will be seen dashing from cover to cover. They love to feed in our garden at night. Only the reedbuck outnumber the dik-diks in taking up residence in our compound during the night. The green grass in our yard is a big attraction, and I have spotted up to a dozen reedbuck in a single night! The genet, entirely nocturnal, is a regular nightly caller as well. They can pass through any opening large enough to admit their heads. Thus we gave up keeping chickens, as they are notorious poultry killers.

The night life here is quite active. The hyena never fails to make his nightly rounds, leaving his den among the rocks and boulders at the hill where he has spent the day. The hyena is mainly, but not entirely, nocturnal. Soon after dusk we hear his gruesome howl. It begins in a low, hoarse tone and then rises sharply to a high-pitched scream. His horrible laugh, diabolic in sound, is made when he has found some food. The next time we bring home an animal for skinning and butchering, we will be sure to hear it again.

The roar of the lion, which can be heard as far as five miles away, is heard mainly at sunset and before dawn. They hunt mostly at night and often make a kill near our compound. They brought down an impala just before dawn one morning within two hundred yards of our place. The water hole has been the site of many of their kills. I have seen their tracks near our house on several occasions. One night, I spooked one off into the tall grass when I shone the torch on him as he wandered along in our yard.

One of the last ones to arrive at the water hole, around midnight, is the elephant, lumbering along cautiously. He stops now and then to test the air currents with his uplifted trunk for any strange scent—especially man's! The half-burnt grass and the dry brush scratch against his hide as he moves along. When they are nearer, I will hear a rumble issued either through the trunk or mouth, which some call belly rumblings. It is the elephants' way of communicating.

The first two years we lived here, elephants came and pulled up our banana trees, wandering without fear across our compound during the night. There were times when they would arrive before dusk at the water hole, marching along one behind the other in full view of us all. We also have seen them leave after dawn. One morning I climbed up a tree standing between the compound and the water hole for a better view of them drinking. Before long they gathered under the tree I was on! I had my camera, but dared not take a picture for fear they might hear it. Then one of them got my scent and froze. Slowly his trunk came up and could easily have pulled me out of the tree had he wanted to, but instead elected to pass a message on to the others with a low rumble. Then like shadows they moved off to the forest beyond where they soon were swallowed up from view.

Other night callers are the bush pig, the cheetah, the wild dog, and the silver-backed jackal. They have all been seen on the plot at one time or another. A pack of wild dogs had a den less than a mile away. They are not very welcome in any community, as game will move out when they move in. The jackal is less of a problem. His screaming yell followed by yaps causes no alarm, as will the clicking or jibber of the wild dog.

The rhino is not a stranger in the neighborhood. This is his stamping ground. One night I was awakened by something squealing. Sounded almost like a pig. Getting up, I went out to check. There in the light of the torch stood a rhino next to my office. With a few grunts and snorts he moved off. Another night, a loud bellow came from outside our bedroom window. Checking it out, I found a hippo in the riverbed not twenty yards away! He had wandered up from the lake. They feed during the night and will forage sometimes several miles away from their aquatic haunts. They will eat the fruit of the sausage tree which grow nearby and on the station as well.

When morning comes, this being the best part of my day, without going far I can sight the impala, Grant gazelle, and hartebeest. In a few hours, they will disappear among the palm trees seeking shade from the blazing sun. The small Thomson gazelle seldom comes here but instead remains on the flats, less than a mile from here. Buffalo have also been spotted from the station in the early hours. They quickly move for cover in the tall grass and dense underbrush growing along the riverbed and near the marsh. There are niches here that man must be very careful about when out strolling. Too many have had the misfortune of disturbing an old bull when out looking for *kuni* and thus became his victim.

As the fruit of the fig tree ripens, vervet monkeys arrive and take up residence. They chatter, scold, and even threaten when approached too closely. The baboons feed on buds of the acacia trees and on flowers of the sausage trees, as well as on seedpods of our huge baobab (which has a girth of fifty-six feet)! The noisy banded mongoose associates very well with the baboon. Under our sausage tree a pack of them will be scratching among the dead leaves for insects, while the troop of baboons will be feeding on the fallen flowers. The mongooses are usually ignored completely by the baboons.

When I am strolling along at eventide on our track which leads out to the main road, various species of birds materialize before my eyes. The ostrich, guinea fowl, crested crane, bustard, hammerkop, hornbill, sand grouse, dove, francolin, hoopoe, wagtail, marabou stork, secretary bird, vulture, eagle, and hawk are just a few of those seen. Plus the songsters that hide among the trees and flowering shrubs, singing for you, if you only listen.

Looking to the northeast on a clear evening or after a rain, I see Mount Kilimanjaro. Its snowy peak now appears pink as it reflects the last light of the sun. As I return to the station, the pyramidal hills are to my left and the palm forest to my right. What a panoramic view! Ahead of me the escarpment is switching from blue to purple as the sun bids farewell to the valley. The lake at the base is a silver ribbon, and palm trees in the foreground are casting long shadows. Doves are cooing softly, even mournfully. How peaceful and serene! In the western sky there are now red and yellow streaks painted on some clouds by the sun as it slips out of sight. Flamingos, winging their way from Lake Burungi to settle for the night on Lake Manyara, add a pinkish hue to the darkening mountains.

This concentration of wildlife was mine to view throughout the fifteen years we lived alongside the Tarangire River between the Great North Road and Lake Manyara at the northern edge of the Mbugwe flats. I could not have wished for a better spot! When I first saw the site and chose it for our home, I never dreamt of all it would offer me. I, who love the wild and the untamed, received all I could ever ask for. Life was never monotonous at any time. There was just so much to see!

I will always remember this place! Years will not erase the wonderful memories I have of this portion of the Tanganyika bush. If a section in heaven will contain this for me, I will be most grateful to the Maker.

171